THE SPIRITUAL POWER OF RUSSIAN IMPERIAL STATEHOOD

ALEKSEY Yu. SALOMATIN

Monography

Academus Publishing
2025

Academus Publishing, Inc.

1999 S, Bascom Avenue, Suite 700 Campbell CA 95008
Website: www.academuspublishing.com
E-mail: info@academuspub.com

© Publisher, Academus Publishing, Inc., 2025

The right of Salomatin A.Yu. — Doctor of Law, Doctor of History, Professor, Corresponding Member of the International Academy of Comparative Law, Head of the Department of Theory of State and Law and Political Science at Penza State University

Translated (from Russian) by artificial intelligence tools. The publisher has carried out technical editing. However, the text may contain translation inaccuracies, typos and artifacts. We would be grateful for feedback to the publisher.

Reviewers:
Bakhlov I.V. — Doctor of Political Science, Professor, Head of the Department of General History, Political Science and Regional Studies at N.P. Ogarev Mordovian State University; Zakharova M.V. — Candidate of Law, Doctor of Public Law (France), Corresponding Member of the International Academy of Comparative Law, Associate Professor of the Department of Theory of State and Law at O.E. Kutafin Moscow State Law Academy

ISBN 10: 1 4946 0029 3
ISBN 13: 978 1 4946 0029 7
DOI 10.31519/monography_1165

The population of every more or less large and successful state has a certain spiritual core around which its social activity is built. For Russia, in our opinion, the basic values of such a spiritual core were commitment to the conservative Orthodox tradition and collectivism, supplemented by a third constantly developing value — the imperial-Eurasian worldview. The chronological framework of the monograph covers the period from Kievan-Novgorod Rus to the present day.

The book will be useful not only for researchers and university teachers, but also for students studying in programs for training lawyers, political scientists, and historians.

CONTENTS

To the reader 4

Essay 1. The emergence of Orthodoxy as a way of life
and thought in Kievan Rus 5

Essay 2. The Orthodox state, peasant-collectivist and conciliar-oriented society
in the era of Muscovy 22

Essay 3. The gradual secularization of the spiritual collectivist
code in the Russian Empire,
18th — early 20th centuries 60

Essay 4. Radicalization and subsequent stabilization
of spiritual life in Soviet and post-Soviet Russia 114

Conclusion 158

Bibliography 161

TO THE READER

The population of every more or less large and successful state has a certain spiritual core around which its social activity is built. It is this core that helps to develop the economy and political system, repel external aggression, and resist internal turmoil. This core is not a constant in itself. It is inevitably adjusted under the influence of circumstances, but nevertheless does not change its inner essence.

For Russia, in our opinion, the basic values of such a spiritual core were adherence to the conservative Orthodox tradition and collectivism, complemented by a third constantly evolving value — the imperial-Eurasian worldview. Commitment to Orthodoxy was formed gradually, in the struggle against paganism in Kievan Rus' and Novgorod Rus', and finally took shape during the Tatar-Mongol rule, and then in Muscovite Rus' in a conservative, isolationist variant that did not allow any concessions to Catholicism, which only strengthened the state and society. Collectivism also developed mainly after the 13th century, when the center of economic life shifted to the forest zone of North-Eastern Rus with its less favorable conditions. Somewhat later, imperial consciousness began to take hold.

People who had migrated from the relatively small area of Muscovy to the east and south began to feel, from the 17th century onwards, that they were part of a great imperial whole, to which numerous local peoples aspired. This feeling apparently began to take shape after the Time of Troubles in the early 17th century. It was this feeling that helped to preserve the vast country after 1917 and after 1991. Can we count on it in the future? Apparently, yes. But at the same time, we should not abandon the lessons of the past, and we should not be short-sighted in hoping that the spiritual core does not need to be cared for by citizens and the state. On the contrary, the era of turbulent globalization forces us to be extremely attentive to foreign ideas and propaganda myths, defending the truth of our history.

Essay 1
THE ESTABLISHMENT OF ORTHODOXY AS A WAY OF LIFE AND THINKING IN KIEV-NOVGOROD RUS

The question of the ethnogenesis of the Eastern Slavs is highly controversial due to the lack of reliable sources. It seems reasonable to agree with the very approximate estimates that the Slavic ethnic group separated from the vast Indo-European community in the 2nd millennium BC and the first half of the 1st millennium BC, and its division into three branches (western, southern, and eastern) is associated with the 5th–8th centuries AD.[1]

The view that the creation of the East Slavic state was not a single act of will on the part of the Varangians, the newcomers, but rather a process that stretched over more than a century (from the end of the 9th century) seems quite logical and reasonable. Until the reign of Svyatoslav and Olga, the Russian lands could not be called a unified state (2). Numerous tribal "chiefdoms" needed to be united, and this task was taken on by the Varangian leaders and their druzhinas. Oleg united the northern territories of the Slovenes, Krivichs, and their Finno-Ugric neighbors with the political entity in the Middle Dnieper region and made a number of "Slavic peoples" of Southeast Europe (Drevlyans, Severians, Radimichs) his vassals. His successor, Igor, further expanded the territory under Kiev's control in the south. Later, Olga directly subjugated the land of the Drevlyans to Kiev. Svyatoslav conquered the Vyatichi, and by the end of the 10th century, Vladimir began to rule all of Rus through governors (sons), which marked the completion of the formation of the state territory (3).

---

[1] Spitsyn, E. Yu. Ancient and Medieval Rus' in the 9th–17th Centuries. Moscow: Conceptual, 2021. pp. 8, 13.

[2] Korolev, A. S. On the role of the Varangian princes in the formation of the ancient Russian state // Teacher. XXI century. 2009.№ 4. pp. 206–213.

[3] Gorsky, A. A. The emergence of Russian statehood and the "calling of the Varangians" // Bulletin of Moscow University. Series 8. History. 2012.№ 5. P. 15.

Moreover, we cannot in any way equate this territory with modern Ukraine, since, firstly, modern Ukraine is only two decades old and has not yet been able to achieve normal internal political stability, and, secondly, the union of Slavic tribes had a wider habitat, and it was organized around two economic and geographical centers — Kiev and Novgorod, which ensured profitable trade "from the Varangians to the Greeks." In other words, Kiev, for all its importance, could not engage in international trade without Novgorod!

It is noteworthy that in this intermediate state between statehood and non-statehood, the spiritual life of the Eastern Slavs developed within the framework of paganism until the end of the 10th century. As Procopius of Caesarea pointed out in the 6th century, "they believe that one of the gods, the creator of lightning, is the lord of all, and they sacrifice bulls to him and perform other sacred rites... They revere rivers and nymphs and all kinds of other deities, offering sacrifices to them all and using these sacrifices to perform divinations." Considering the vast territory occupied by the Eastern Slavs, it is likely that there was no common Slavic pantheon of pagan gods, but most likely the most revered deities among them were: **Perun**, the god of lightning, thunder, and war; **Veles**, the god of wisdom, cattle breeding, and trade; the god of wind and whirlwind, **Stribog**; the god of fire, **Svarog**; the goddess of fertility and prosperity, **Mokosh**; and the four hypostases (depending on the season) of the Sun: **Yarilo** (spring–summer), **Horos** (summer–autumn), **Yasen** (autumn–winter) and **Dazhbog** (winter–spring) (1). The fragmentation and substantive "underdevelopment" of Slavic mythology clearly hindered state building, which was keenly felt by Grand Prince Vladimir.

With the adoption of Orthodox Christianity in 988,
Our homeland received powerful spiritual support. The church organization was taking shape: "In addition to Novgorod the Great, St. Vladimir established bishoprics in other cities of Rus: Belgorod (near Kiev), Polotsk, Vladimir Volynsky, Chernigov, and Turov" (2). By 1170, there were already 11 dioceses, and the Novgorod bishops had the rank of archbishop.

---

[1] Spitsyn E. Yu. Ancient and Medieval Rus... p. 18.

[2] Petrusko, V. I. Essays on the History of the Russian Church from Ancient Times to the Middle of the 15th Century. Moscow, 2019. p. 31.

They were subordinate to the Metropolitan of Kiev, not to the Patriarch, as was customary in the Byzantine Church (1).

Unlike Western countries, where secular and ecclesiastical authorities were in fierce competition with each other, **Kievan-Novgorod Rus** did not experience conflicts that were destructive to society, but proceeded from **a "symphony of powers."** Good relations in the early stages may have been facilitated by the fact that the Russian Church, represented by its highest hierarchs, was formed from among the subjects of the Byzantine emperor, i.e., "newcomers," and could not be an independent center of power, although it enjoyed high respect. The only known exception is the appointment by the Prince of Kiev and the Council of Russian Bishops in 1051 of the Russian priest and outstanding scholar **Hilarion** as Metropolitan, and the only acute conflict between Byzantium and the Russian princes involving the church dates back to the middle of the 12th century.

Then, Byzantine Emperor Manuel Comnenus, gathering a coalition against the Hungarian king who was hostile to him, faced opposition from the Kiev prince Izyaslav: the latter "persuaded the Council of Russian Bishops to elect his protégé, the monk **Clement,** a native of Smolensk, as metropolitan," bypassing Constantinople. "This arbitrary action caused confusion in the Russian Church, intensified the enmity between the princes, and led to a schism between the Kiev Metropolis and the Patriarchate, which continued with few interruptions for nine years. An influential minority of bishops, mainly consisting of citizens of Byzantium, claimed that the appointment was uncanonical and invalid. A similar point of view was held by those Russian princes who were either allies of the empire or, for other reasons, considered Izyaslav their enemy. Only after his death in 1154 did the people of Kiev agree to accept the metropolitan sent from **Constantinople**

The not entirely independent status of Kiev-Novgorod Orthodoxy corresponded to the youth of East Slavic statehood. Nevertheless, the Byzantine model of Christianity played an important cultural and civilizational role. Monasteries and churches were centers for maintaining literacy. Spiritual Figures — Illarion, Nestor, Silvestr, Daniil, Kliment

---

[1] Petrusko, V. I. Essays on the History of the Russian Church from Ancient Times to the Middle of the 15th Century. Moscow, 2019. p. 51.

[2] Obolensky, D. The Byzantine Commonwealth of Nations. Six Portraits. Moscow, 2012. P. 243.

Smolyatich, Kirill of Turov (1) formulated the most important socio-political tasks and became the first chroniclers and ideologists of our homeland. New church holidays began to enter the lives of our compatriots. Two of them — **Nikola Vesny** (May 22) and **Nikola Zimny** (December 19), dedicated to the transfer of the relics of St. Nicholas the Wonderworker to the Italian city of Bari and his death, have been celebrated since the end of the 11th century, especially widely in Russian Orthodoxy.

The construction of religious buildings also spread widely in the East Slavic lands. Under Prince Vladimir, the construction of **the** stone **Cathedral of the Mother of God**, the main temple of the country, was completed in 996. Under Yaroslav the Wise, the construction of **St. Sophia Cathedral** was carried out. Under him, in 1051, **the Kiev-Pechersk Monastery** was founded on the site where the first monks-hermits lived in underground caves.

Prince Izyaslav Yaroslavich was a particularly generous patron of the monastery, donating the hill above the caves to it. **The Assumption Cathedral** was built on this hill and consecrated in 1189 (Fig. 1.1).

Fig. 1.1. Holy Dormition Kiev-Pechersk Lavra. Modern view

---

[1] Bohanov, A. N., Morozova, L. E., Rakhmatullin, M. A., Sakharov, A. N., Shestakov, V. A. History of Russia from Ancient Times to the Present Day / ed. by A. N. Sakharov. Moscow, 2016. pp. 197–205.

Fig. 1.2. St. Sophia Cathedral in Novgorod. Modern view

The first Russian architects and artists — Alipy Pechersky, the Reverend Gregory, and Agapit — studied under the Greek architects and icon painters who created this model of church architecture. Other Russian monasteries took abbots from the Kiev-Pechersk Lavra. Future bishops of the Russian Church were also educated here.

Among the monks of Pechersk, we can recall the names of Saints Stephen of Volodymyr-Volynsky, Nikita and Nifont of Novgorod, and Simon of Vladimir-Suzdal [1]. As for Kiev itself, during its heyday under Yaroslav the Wise (1019–1054), there were about 400 churches here

Novgorod has preserved the most churches from **the pre-Mongol period, which indirectly testifies to its important and favorable strategic position. St. Sophia Cathedral**, built in 1050, is the oldest of all the surviving churches in Russia (Fig. 1.2).

---

[1] Petrusko V. I. Essays on the History of the Russian Church... p. 56.

[2] History of Russia from ancient times to the present day... p. 112.

[3] All 13 pre-Mongol churches of Veliky Novgorod and its surroundings. URL: https://globeofrussia.ru/2016/01/vse-13-domongolskih-hramov-velikogo-novgoroda-i-okrestnostey/ (accessed on May 1, 2021).

Fig. 1.3. St. George's Cathedral of the Yuriev Monastery

Fig. 1.4. "Saint George" — the temple icon of St. George's Cathedral, one of the oldest in Russia

Grand Prince Yaroslav the Wise and Princess Irina, who had arrived from Kiev, as well as Prince Vladimir Yaroslavich of Novgorod, were present at its foundation. Slightly younger is **St. George's Cathedral of the Yuriev Monastery** (Figs. 1.3, 1.4), laid in 1119 on the initiative of Grand Prince Mstislav I Vladimirovich. This temple became a burial place for Russian princes and Novgorod posadniks, as well as abbots. Unlike most religious buildings erected by the official authorities, **the Anthony Monastery** and its **Cathedral of the Nativity of the Mother of God** were created in 1117 by a private individual, Anthony the Roman. Legend links him to Italy, but it is possible that as a merchant he came from the Holy Roman Empire of the German Nation or was sent by the Kiev-Pechersk Lavra to strengthen Kiev's influence in Novgorod (Fig. 1.5).

Pskov, which until the mid-13th century was under the influence of Novgorod and defended its western borders, was famous for its devotion to Orthodox Christianity: in ancient times, there were 12 monasteries along the banks of the Velikaya River, which divides the city into two parts. Among the most significant structures is **the Cathedral of St. John the Baptist of the Ioannovsky Convent** (Fig. 1.6), which was built in the first half of the 12th century and became the burial place of the Pskov princesses.

Fig. 1.5. Cathedral of the Nativity of the Mother of God of the Antoniev Monastery. Modern view

Fig. 1.6. Cathedral of St. John the Baptist in Pskov. Modern view

Fig. 1.7. TransFiguration Cathedral of the Mirozhsky Monastery in Pskov. Modern view

Fig. 1.8. TransFiguration Cathedral (Pereslavl-Zalessky)

Fig. 1.9. Church of Boris and Gleb in Kideksha near Suzdal

The Transfiguration Cathedral of the **Mirozhsky Monastery** (founded in 1153) preserved unique pre-Mongol frescoes by Greek masters, as well as the monastery's holy relic — the icon **of the Sign of the Most Holy Mother of God**, which helped the inhabitants during the plague epidemic in 1567 (1) (Fig. 1.7).

In 1038, Boyar Efrem founded the Borisoglebsky Monastery on the banks of the Tvertsa River in **the Tver region**. His relics were found during the reign of Ivan the Terrible, and the monastery itself, after a period of decline and desolation, experienced a revival in the second half of the 18th century. However, Tver itself was founded only in 1181 and was originally part of the Suzdal Principality, and then the Pereslavl-Zalessky Principality. Its heyday began in the middle of the 13th century under Prince Yaroslav Yaroslavich.

In the northeast of Rus, whose capital successively moved from the oldest city, **Rostov** (mentioned in the chronicles in 862), to **Suzdal** (1125), and then to **Vladimir** (in the mid-12th century), Orthodox Christianity struggled to gain a foothold until the end of the 11th century, and the episcopal see was only truly established under Leontius in the 1070s, who was martyred by pagans (2).

In Rostov, **the Assumption Cathedral**, which began construction in 1161–1163, became the largest temple in the Rostov-Suzdal region, which apparently symbolized the ambition of Rostov residents over the inhabitants of neighboring settlements (3). However, it has been almost completely destroyed and rebuilt at the beginning of the 16th century. On the other hand, **the TransFiguration Cathedral in Pereslavl-Zalessky**, a city founded by Yuri Dolgoruky with great difficulty on marshy ground (4) and surrounded by very long walls stretching 2.5 km (only Kiev and Smolensk had longer walls, stretching 3.5 km). This same outstanding prince built **the Church of Boris and Gleb** in the village of Kideksha, 4 km from Suzdal, which has largely survived to this day (Figs. 1.8, 1.9).

---

[1] Ten churches in Pskov are on the UNESCO list. Why are they a must-see? URL: ttps://tass.ru/v-strane/6664403 (accessed: 01.05.2021).

[2] Fomina, T. Yu. The Formation and Development of the North-Eastern Russian Bishoprics (late 10th–13th centuries) // Paleorossiya. Ancient Rus: in time, personalities, ideas. 2016. No. 6. Pp. 387–392.

[3] Melnik A. G. The proud people of Rostov: the self-awareness of the inhabitants of Rostov at the end of the 11th – first third of the 13th centuries // Yaroslavl Pedagogical Bulletin. 2016. No. 3. P. 282.

[4] Zagraevsky S. V. On the question of the capital of North-Eastern Rus: Pereslavl-Zalessky under Yuri Dolgoruky, Bogolyubovo under Andrei Bogolyubsky // Materials of the XX Interregional Local History Conference (April 17, 2015). Vladimir. 2016. Pp. 296–306.

Fig. 1.10. Cathedral of the Assumption of the Blessed Virgin Mary in Vladimir

Under Andrei Bogolyubsky and Vsevolod the Big Nest in North-Eastern Rus, the time came for Vladimir to flourish. **The Assumption Cathedral** was built there **in** 1158–1160, later becoming the main temple of Rus (Fig. 1.10), and **the Dmitrievsky Cathedral (**1190s) in honor of Dmitry of Thessaloniki, the heavenly patron of Grand Prince Vsevolod the Big Nest.

The period of prosperity for Bogolyubovo, founded 10 km from Vladimir at the site of the apparition of the Mother of God to Prince Andrei Bogolyubsky, was shorter. The city, founded in 1158, had two fortification systems: an inner white-stone perimeter of about 1.5 km and an outer wooden and earthen rampart 2.9 km long, which exceeds the size of Vladimir, Yuryev-Polsky, and Suzdal.

To this day, parts of the earthen ramparts, the lower parts of the walls and pillars, and the fortifications have been partially preserved, while only the base of **the Church of the Nativity of the Mother of God remains**, on which a Baroque-style church was built in the mid-18th century (Fig. 1.11).

At the same time, **the Church of the Intercession of the Holy Virgin on the Nerl River**, located 1.5 km away at the confluence of this river with the Klyazma River, with a panorama of Bogolyubov and Vladimir, has survived to this day mainly in its original form (the original interior paintings have been lost) (Fig. 1.12).

Fig. 1.11. Church of the Nativity of the Virgin Mary and the remains of Andrei Bogolyubsky's castle

Fig. 1.12. Church of the Intercession of the Holy Virgin on the Nerl

Fig. 1.13. Transfiguration Monastery. Modern view

This structure on an artificial hill with a foundation measuring more than 5 m is considered one of the outstanding monuments of world art (1).

Yaroslavl, the first Russian city on the Volga River at the confluence of the Kotorosl River, was founded in the 11th century (the officially recognized date is 1010). In the 11th–12th centuries, it was just a small border town in the Rostov-Suzdal region, and it was during this period that **the Petropavlovsky (Petrovsky)** and **Spaso-Preobrazhensky monasteries** were founded outside the city (Fig. 1.13). The first stone buildings in the city date back to the reign of Vsevolod the Big Nest's son, **Konstantin.** He founded the first educational institution in North-Eastern Rus' within the walls of the Spaso-Preobrazhensky Monastery — **the Grigorievsky Zavtor** (named after Gregory the Theologian, one of the fathers of the Church of the 4th century). The school had a library, a workshop for copying manuscripts, and taught Greek and other languages, as well as chronicling history. Konstantin Vsevolodovich also rebuilt **the Assumption Cathedral** in stone **in** 1215–1219, and after his death, the TransFiguration Cathedral (1216–1224) was completed, rebuilt from scratch.

---

[1] Grabar, I. E. On Russian Architecture: Research, Preservation of Monuments. Moscow, 1969. P. 47.

After a fire in the early 16th century, in the image and likeness of the cathedrals of the Moscow Kremlin (1).

In general, by the first third of the 13th century, not only had numerous church buildings been constructed in Kievan Rus', attracting believers, but a fairly extensive church organization had also developed. The bishops were assisted in their administration by their colleagues, **the presbyters,** who, however, did not manage to form a clear bureaucratic hierarchy, as was the case in the Byzantine Empire. In addition, given the enormous size of Russian dioceses, episcopal vicars played an important role. They "were usually located in large cities of the diocese, where there were independent princes or princely **vicars."** These individuals "acted locally, almost completely replacing the bishop, possessing judicial power and lacking only the right to perform ordinations." (2) At the same time the collectors of church tithes were purely secular Figures.

The church was supported by monasteries, which were mainly princely. "Of the 68 monasteries known in Russia in the pre-Mongol period, two-thirds were built by princes and other private individuals. The princes founded monasteries for the repose of their souls, built churches around them, made generous donations, and from the beginning of the 12th century, endowed them with land, **but considered these monasteries their property and disposed of them at their discretion."** (3)

Secular power undoubtedly underwent a certain evolution during the 11th to mid-13th centuries. The reign **of Yaroslav the Wise** (1019–1054) was the happiest period in terms of the unity of the vast Kiev-Novgorod lands. In some ways, it bears analogy to the empire **of Charlemagne** (768–814) in Western Europe.

However, this is an external, speculative comparison of two reigns lasting 35 and 46 years, respectively, in different historical eras and under different geopolitical conditions. Charlemagne's empire was created in the course of harsh, multidirectional expansion and was accompanied by violent Christianization with the blessing and support of the ramified apparatus of the Catholic Church.

---

[1] Spaso-Preobrazhensky Monastery. URL: https://city-yaroslavl.ru/tourism/places/spaso-preobraxhenskiy-monastyr (accessed: 17.09.2021).

[2] Petrusko, V. I. Essays on the History of the Russian Church... pp. 52–53.

[3] Ibid. p. 54.

Kievan Rus' consisted of a dozen or so tribal unions or territorial-political communities that had closer ethnic ties than in the West and were not forced to unite by a powerful church organization.

The resulting state (Kievan Rus or Russian Land) was hardly a federation of "city-states" with a veche system (1). Its history should hardly be likened to the templates of European feudalism, or, conversely, artificially "rejuvenated" in terms of socio-economic and political development, attributing to it a "pre-feudal" state.

It is important to understand that over the course of 80–100 years (roughly from 1054 to 1132), the process of territorial fragmentation progressed here, and at the same time, it was apparently not yet complete: "strong centrifugal tendencies were always counterbalanced by equally powerful centripetal forces, in particular, the nominal but nevertheless supreme authority of the Grand Prince of Kiev and the Russian Orthodox Church, whose metropolitan see was still located in Kiev" (2).

"In the 12th century, twelve lands were formed on the territory of Rus: Kiev, Pereyaslav, Chernigov, Volhynia, Galicia, Smolensk, Suzdal (sometimes called Rostov), Novgorod, Polotsk, Ryazan, Murom, and Pinsk... Contrary to popular belief, they did not repeat the borders of the pre-state communities of the preceding 9th–10th centuries... In most lands, certain branches of the Rurik dynasty became established. If in the 11th century princes, as a rule, changed the volost in which they ruled several times during their lifetime (usually at the will of the supreme ruler, the Prince of Kiev), then by the middle of the 12th century, the dynasties that had formed by that time "settled" in one volost or another (3).

Many works of Old Russian literature attempted to promote **the patriotic idea of uniting the Old Russian lands**, the most famous of which is
The Tale of Igor's Campaign, attributed to the Kiev thousand commander Peter Borisovich (4).

---

[1] Froyanov, I. Ya. Ancient Rus' of the 9th–13th Centuries. Popular Movements. Princely and Veche Power. Moscow, 2012.

[2] Spitsyn E. Yu. Ancient and Medieval Rus... p. 97.

[3] Gorsky, A. Medieval Rus. What the sources say. Moscow, 2016. P. 44.

[4] Rybakov, B. A. Russian chroniclers and the author of The Tale of Igor's Campaign. Moscow, 1972. P. 515.

"The campaign of Prince Igor of Severia against the Polovtsians was of a private nature, but the author of The Tale turns this episode into a pan-Russian event... Even the geographical action of The Tale unfolds over a vast area from Novgorod the Great in the north to Tmutarakan (Taman Peninsula) in the south, from the Volga in the east to Galich and the Carpathians in the west." (1)

However, even the most heartfelt calls for unity could not help. Civil strife multiplied, because "the sons did not want to give power to the older princes, their uncles, and the latter did not allow their nephews to come to power, putting their sons in their place, even though they were younger" (2). By the beginning of the 13th century, there were about 50 princely domains in Rus.

***

The early pages of Russian statehood (late 9th to early 13th centuries) were marked by **the consolidation of secular power**, which was predominantly regional in nature. Many ancient Russian sources mention the unification of the East Slavic lands, but under the influence of objective regionalization processes, **the idea of patriotism** was **eroded.** Young Orthodox Christianity was not yet able to have a significant say, as it bore the mark of the organizational and personnel influence of the distant Byzantine Patriarchate and could not occupy a sufficiently independent position in relation to secular rulers (Scheme 1.1).

A third important element is added to **the** emerging **princely-Orthodox spiritual core** of the Old Russian people: **peasant collectivism**, since the complex natural and climatic conditions of the forest-steppe zone require collective economic efforts.

Undoubtedly, as the northeastern forest and marshlands, far from the dangerous steppe nomads, were colonized, the scale of these collective efforts would only increase.

The Tatar-Mongol invasion not only caused enormous material damage, but also weakened the Russian lands organizationally. For example, after the reign of Alexander Nevsky, northeastern Russia broke up into many principalities: Galich, Kostroma, Gorodets, Dmitrov, Moscow, Starodub,

---

[1] Sosenkov F. S. Ideas of the unity of the Russian land in the heroic epic of the 12th–14th centuries. // Current problems of Russian law. 2015.№ 3. P. 10.

[2] History of Russia from ancient times to the present day... P. 139.

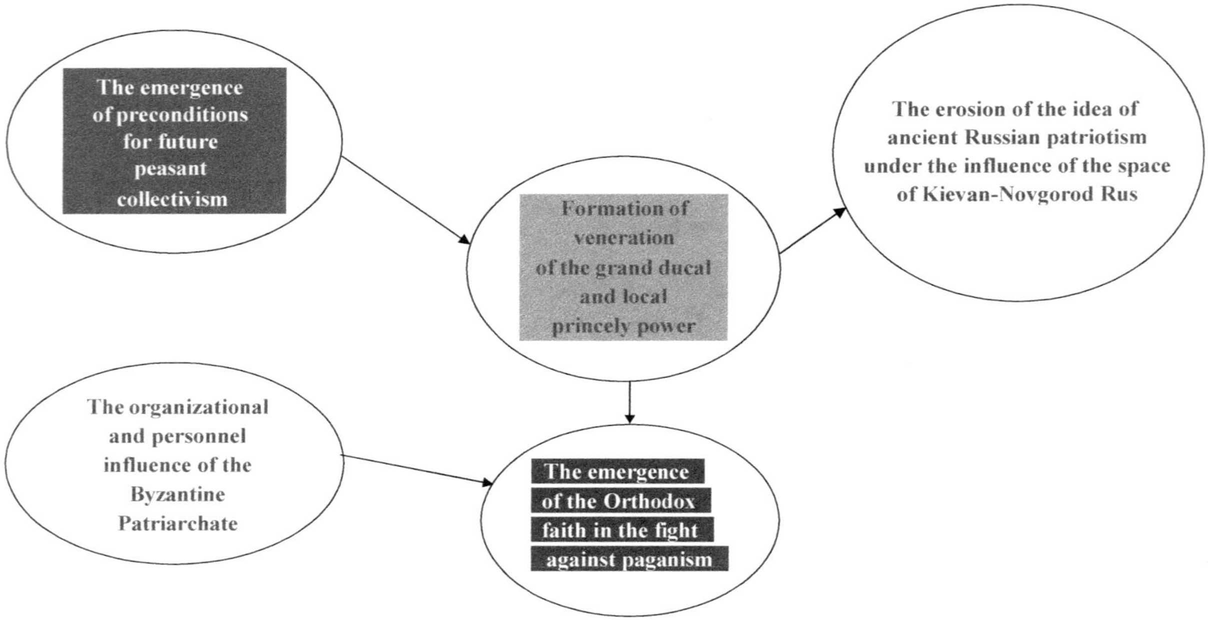

Diagram 1.1. The spiritual core of Kievan Rus' and Novgorod Rus' at the time of the Tatar-Mongol invasion (first third of the 13th century)

Suzdal, Tver, Pereyaslav, Rostov, Uglich, Yaroslavl. At the same time, the Orthodox clergy managed to strengthen their position under the Tatars and Mongols. "The Old Russian church organization survived the Tatar-Mongol invasion of 1237–1240 with fewer losses than is claimed in historiography. The death of the episcopate is recorded in the pages of Old Russian chronicles only in the context of the siege and plundering of Russian cities; by remaining loyal to the Mongol authorities, the bishops preserved not only their lives but also their social status." (1)

---

[1] Fomina, T. Yu. The Episcopal Structure of Rus' during the Mongol-Tatar Invasion of 1237–1240. // Zolotoordynskoe Obozrenie. 2019.№ 7. P. 261.

Essay 2
THE ORTHODOX STATE, THE PEASANT-COLLECTIVIST AND CONCILIATORY-ORIENTED SOCIETY IN THE ERA OF MOSCOW RUS

As with the unification of Russian lands, the 14th century was of fateful significance for the development of Orthodoxy. It was then that North-Eastern Rus began to recover from the devastating Tatar-Mongol catastrophe of the mid-13th century. This was reflected in the establishment of a metropolis, the construction of monasteries, and missionary activity.

It is understandable that, due to the unprecedented devastation of Southern Rus, the Kiev metropolitans felt insecure and preferred other, more peaceful cities. In particular, **Metropolitan Cyril**, nominated on the initiative of the powerful Galician prince Daniel, traveled extensively throughout his church possessions, but preferred Vladimir on the Klyazma as his unofficial residence. His successor, **Metropolitan Maxim,** eventually moved with his entire clergy to the Suzdal region in 1299.

The next spiritual leader, **Metropolitan Peter**, a native of Volhynia, whom his contemporaries compared to the great saints of the 4th century (Basil the Great, Gregory the Theologian, and John Chrysostom), was a supporter of a strong Russian state and the leading role of Moscow. Elevated to the rank of Metropolitan of Kiev and All Russia, he moved to Vladimir after a year in Kiev, and in 1325 to Moscow. In the conflicts between Tver and Moscow, Peter consistently supported the latter, which made him a target of persecution by the Tver authorities and their church minions.

Moscow's rise to prominence aroused jealousy on the part of its western rival, the Grand Duchy of Lithuania, which had risen sharply in the mid-14th century. The cherished desire of the Lithuanian rulers was to "persuade the Byzantine authorities either.

to transfer the metropolitan see to Lithuania, or at least to establish a separate metropolis in their country." Lithuanian ambitions presented the Byzantine emperors and patriarchs with a difficult choice. "Tradition, administrative simplicity, and respect for the authority and financial **capabilities of the Moscow princes spoke in favor of the pro-Moscow decision."** (1) However, the Lithuanian side blackmailed Constantinople by saying that if its request was ignored, the Lithuanian pagans might convert to Catholicism rather than Orthodox Christianity. The Russian-Lithuanian dispute, which began in the 1350s, was only resolved at the beginning of the 15th century, when the Lithuanian diocese was finally subordinated to Moscow. By this time, the Moscow lands had finally demonstrated their defensive capabilities and statehood.

In their rapidly growing capital, there were apparently already four monasteries in the first half of the 14th century: **Spassky in the Kremlin, Bogoyavlensky in Posad, Krutitsky,** and **Danilov on the Moskva River.** (2) Later, other monasteries were built in the Kremlin: Chudov, **Mikhailo-Arkhangelsky, Voznesensky,** and **Afanasyevsky** (founded in 1365, 1386, and 1385, respectively).

At the same time, it must be acknowledged that during the era of Tatar-Mongol rule, the church strengthened its position in relation to princely power thanks to the benevolent attitude of the religiously tolerant khans. Its transformation "into a full-fledged feudal institution took place only during the era of Horde rule and with the active participation of the khan's power." At that time, it "acquired a multitude of various immunities..." (3)

During the 14th century, intensive construction of monasteries began in North-Eastern Rus, which, unlike in the previous historical era of Kievan-Novgorod Rus, were organized not only in the suburbs of cities, but also in rural areas, becoming centers of economic consolidation and Orthodox piety. Thanks to Sergius of Radonezh, **the Trinity-Sergius Lavra** became the most famous such center (Fig. 2.1).

---

[1] Obolensky, D. The Byzantine Commonwealth of Nations. Six Byzantine Portraits. Moscow, 2012. P. 279.

[2] Tikhomirov, M. N. Ancient Moscow. Moscow, 1947. P. 151.

[3] Galimov, T. R. The Influence of the Horde on the Canonical and Legal Status of the Metropolitan See and the Russian Church in the Second Half of the 13th and Early 14th Centuries. // Ancient Rus: In Time, Personalities, and Ideas. 2017. № 8. P. 435.

Fig. 2.1. Trinity-Sergius Lavra. Modern view

Fig. 2.2. St. Sergius of Radonezh

According to various sources, **Saint Sergius of Radonezh** was born in 1314 or 1322 in the Rostov Principality into a family of noble but impoverished boyars. Around 1340, he and his older brother founded a small church and hut, which later grew into the Trinity-Sergius Lavra. However, his older brother soon left him, moving to the Epiphany Monastery in Moscow, where he became its abbot and confessor to Grand Prince Simeon (Fig. 2.2). Monks gradually gathered around Sergius and persuaded him to become their abbot, which happened sometime between 1354 and 1356. The monastery grew. Sergius's authority, who by his personal example performed various necessary tasks (milling wheat, sowing flour, baking prosphora, cooking kutia, making candles), was strengthened. News of his righteous life and the miracles he performed attracted people to him and increased donations to the monastery.

The monastery cared for the poor, and the powerful sought Sergius's advice, including Grand Prince Dmitry Donskoy. Metropolitan Alexius tried to persuade the reverend abbot to become his successor, but to no avail. With the active participation of St. Sergius, several well-known monasteries were founded: **the Annunciation Monastery on the Kirzhach River** (Fig. 2.3), **the Spaso-Andronikov Monastery on the Yauza River** (Fig. 2.4), **the Borisoglebsky Monastery near Rostov** (Fig. 2.5), and **the Simonov Monastery in Moscow** (Fig. 2.6). "The disciples and spiritual children of the Venerable Sergius founded (both during his lifetime and after his death) up to 40 monasteries; from these, in turn, came the founders of approximately 50 more monasteries." St. Sergius died in 1392 (or 1397) at the age of 72 (or 78). He is rightly considered the spiritual unifier of the Russian people and the founder of Russian monasticism. He is revered not only by the Orthodox Church, but also by the Catholic Church.

A younger contemporary, friend, and colleague of Sergius of Radonezh was another ascetic, **Stephen of Perm**, who was born in 1340 into the family of a cathedral cleric in Veliky Ustyug. At the age of 20, he took monastic vows at the Monastery of St. Gregory the Theologian in Rostov the Great, one of the centers of learning in Rus. There he mastered the Greek language and became one of the most profound interpreters of Holy Scripture. After some time, he was ordained a priest and began to prepare for preaching among the Zyrian pagans who lived in the vicinity of Veliky Ustyug. Stephen compiled the Zyrian alphabet and translated the Holy Scriptures, which was an unprecedented feat, since.

Fig. 2.3. Blagoveshchensky Monastery (Kirzhach)

Fig. 2.4. Spaso-Andronikov Monastery

Fig. 2.5. Borisoglebsky Monastery in Rostov

Fig. 2.6. Preserved towers of the Simonov Monastery

Fig. 2.7. Stephen of Perm, icon from 1909.

Fig. 2.8. Icon "Zyryanskaya Trinity," painted, according to legend, by Stephen of Perm

Everywhere, church services were conducted in the Slavic language. This preparatory work took at least 15 years (Figs. 2.7, 2.8).

Having received the blessing of the church authorities and a letter of protection from Grand Duke Dmitry Donskoy, in 1379–early 1380, the saint came to Malaya Perm. He began preaching in the area of the modern city of Kotlas, then traveled along the Perm River and built a wooden church dedicated to the Annunciation of the Mother of God in the main Zyrian settlement of Ust-Vym. Overcoming the resistance of local sorcerers, he won the trust of the Zyrians, although he did not completely eradicate paganism. In 1383, he was ordained bishop of Perm, and Ust-Vym became a cathedral city.

Stephen sincerely cared for his new flock. He asked the Grand Duke in Moscow to ensure that officials did not oppress them; he appealed to the authorities in Novgorod to protect honest residents from Novgorod robbers. During times of crop failure and famine, he bought bread in Veliky Ustyug and Vologda for the starving. He asked the Moscow ruler to forgive the Zyrians' tax arrears.

Fig. 2.9. Ensemble of the Belozersk Ferapontov Monastery

Stefan's missionary work continued for 18 years, until his death in 1396. By this time, the Perm diocese had grown to cover a huge territory.

In 1398, **the Reverend Ferapont,** also a native of the Simonov Monastery, organized a monastery nearby, on the shore of Lake Borodavsky. **The Belozersk Ferapontov Monastery** was generously funded by the owner of the local lands, Prince Andrei Dmitrievich of Mozhaisk (Figs. 2.9, 2.10).

Other ascetics also participated in the spiritual guidance of the northern territories. For example, **the Reverend Cyril,** who was born in 1337 in Moscow and took his vows at the Simonov Monastery, eventually became its abbot in 1389. However, he was drawn to the silence of the North, and in 1397 he founded a monastery on the shore of Lake Siversky. He ruled **the Kirillo-Belozersky Monastery** for 30 years until his death in 1427 (Figs. 2.11, 2.12).

Along with active missionary work in the northern territories, a significant event in the monastery's history was the establishment of **the Nikolo-Ugreshsky Monastery** in honor of the victory on Kulikovo Field,

Fig. 2.10. Venerable Ferapont of Belozersk — founder of the Belozersk Ferapont Monastery (17th-century icon)

Fig. 2.11. Venerable Cyril — founder of the Kirillo-Belozersky Monastery (icon painted by Fig. 2.12. Kirillo-Belozersky Monastery

Fig. 2.12. Kirillo-Belozersky Monastery

located on the left bank of the Moskva River near the capital. This place became the object of increased attention from Russian monarchs: it was visited by "Grand Duke Vasily Ioannovich in 1519, Ivan the Terrible in 1546, Tsar Mikhail Fedorovich 9 times, and Tsar Alexei Mikhailovich 13 times" (1). Since the 16th century, there has been "active secularization" of this monastery (as well as others): it concentrated in its hands land, a subjugated population far from its location, and economic privileges. (2)

As is well known, the departure of the Christian Church in both the East and the West from the Christian ideals of selflessness and love provoked protests from many believers, which transformed into various deviations from official doctrine. At the same time, these deviations did not become as widespread and fierce in Russia as they did outside its borders.

It is difficult to agree with the opinion that "the clergy was free from Russian authority, which led to a situation **where the priesthood became superior to the kingdom." The statement that "all decisions of the princes were, as a rule, agreed upon with the bishops and the metropolitan" (3) is also untrue.** Even taking into account the Tatar-Mongols' favorable attitude toward Orthodoxy, the growth of church land ownership, and conflicts between princes, **the influence of Orthodoxy as an organization should not be overestimated.** Unlike the Roman Catholic Church in the West, it lacked strict hierarchical ties and had neither the opportunity nor the power to openly oppose the secular authorities. Hence **the absence of mass discontent with the enriching hierarchs.** Rather, this discontent was localized, inspired by Western influence that came through the Novgorod and Pskov lands.

The Strigolnik sect apparently arose as a negative reaction to the contradictions in the church hierarchy during the struggle between Moscow and the Grand Duchy of Lithuania over the structure of the church. "Participants in the Strigolnik movement (representatives the lower clergy,

---

[1] Golitsyn, N. S. Nikolo-Ugreshsky Monastery (excerpts from an essay) // Cultural Heritage of Russia. 2013. P. 41.

[2] Patyulina N. D. The Nikolo-Ugreshsky Monastery in the socio-political system of the state // News of the Russian State Pedagogical University named after A. I. Herzen. 2008. P. 272–274.

[3] Eremin A. V. The Formation of State and Church Relations in Russia: A Historical and Cultural Analysis // Bulletin of the Moscow State University of Culture and Arts. 2014. P. 39.

artisans, and merchants) opposed the greed and ignorance of the Orthodox clergy, rejected church sacraments, and demanded the right of religious **preaching** for lay people. (1) Due to a lack of factual material, we are unable to determine exactly which foreign ideas influenced the Strigolniks — Bogomilism **or the Albigensians (2),** or perhaps the Hussites. But in any case, there is no reason to speak of the long-term and mass nature of religious dissent in our country.

XV became an important milestone for Russian Orthodoxy, as it marked the complete formation of the ideological and organizational independence of the Moscow metropolitans. **Isidore,** a Byzantine church diplomat and humanist who supported rapprochement with Catholic Rome, became the last church hierarch imposed on Moscow by Constantinople. By signing in 1439 along with the Constantinople religious leadership, **he began to appear as a religious traitor** in the eyes of the Grand Prince of Moscow and the Russian clergy. Immediately after his return from Western Europe and a service at the Cathedral of the Assumption (1441), he was taken into custody. Apparently, with the knowledge of the Grand Prince, the unfortunate signatory was helped to flee to the West, so that the authorities had a free hand in filling the vacancy that had arisen. In 1448, without consulting Constantinople, Moscow was able to elect Bishop **Jonah** of Ryazan (1448–1461) as Metropolitan at the Council of Bishops of Eastern Rus. Jonah became the last hierarch who, holding the title of Metropolitan of Kiev, had a see in Moscow. In 1459, a conciliar decision established a new procedure for electing metropolitans — by the votes of Russian bishops with the consent of the Prince of Moscow, which meant **the de facto autocephaly of the Russian Church.**

The new position of Moscow and the Russian Orthodox Church was confirmed by the theory of "Moscow — the Third Rome".

---

[1] Osipova V. V. Russian sectarianism as a form of religious dissent in the pre-revolutionary period // Public Administration. Electronic Bulletin. 2019. P. 4.

[2] Petrusko, V. I. Essays on the History of the Russian Church from Ancient Times to the Middle of the 15th Century. Moscow, 2019. P. 454.

The abbot of the Pskov Elizarov Monastery, Philotheus, wrote to Grand Duke Vasily III: "All Christian kingdoms have come together in yours, that two Romes have fallen, and the third stands, and the fourth will not be" (1).

In the 15th century, in accordance with the tasks of establishing a centralized Moscow state, intensive monastery and church construction began. For example, on its northeastern borders, 90 km from Nizhny Novgorod down the Volga River, a modest wooden church was founded in 1435 in honor of the Holy Life-Giving Trinity. This monastery existed for only five years before being destroyed by the Khan of Kazan, but it was restored two centuries later. By the 16th century, **the Holy Trinity Makaryevo-Zheltovodsky Monastery** had become not only a center of religious life, but also the venue for the famous Makaryevsky Fair, apparently the largest in Europe.

Thanks to **the Reverend Pafnuty**, who was abbot of the Borovsk Pokrovsky Monastery for 13 years, **the Borovsk Pafnuty Monastery** was founded after 1448 and became widely known. Pafnuty ruled it for about 30 years and was famous for his personal modesty.

Fig. 2.13. Venerable Paphnutius of Borovsk

"He usually ate nothing on Mondays and Fridays, ate only bread on Wednesdays, and on other days he dined with the brethren (Figs. 2.13, 2.14).

He always worked hard: he chopped and carried wood wood, dug the ground for the fence, carried water for watering the plants... In winter he devoted

---

[1] Philotheus. Letter to Grand Prince Vasily on the correction of the sign of the cross and on Sodom's fornication // Anthology of World Political Thought: in 5 vols. Vol. III. Political Thought in Russia: 10th–first half of the 20th century. Moscow, 1997. pp. 151–152.

more time to prayer and reading, and wove nets for fishing (1). Paphnutius was known for his generous assistance to those in need; he could feed a thousand people or more during times of famine, depleting the monastery's supplies. He healed the sick and was respected among the powerful of this world — the appanage princes and the Grand Prince. The holy elder died in 1477 at the age of 82, when the monastery already had 95 monks. On the western outskirts of the Russian lands, the now famous (Holy Dormition) **Pskov-Pechersk Monastery**, one of the largest and most famous in Russia, was founded at the end of the 15th century, 50 km west of the capital of the Pskov region (Fig. 2.15). It began with **the cave church of the Dormition of the Mother of God,** dug out of a sandstone hill by the Reverend Jonah. In the 16th century, under Abbot Kornilii, the monastery was turned into a strong fortress — stone walls were erected (1558–1583), which allowed it to repel attacks by enemies (Poles and Swedes) for 150 years. The monastery is also known for its miraculous icon **of the Dormition of the Most Holy Mother of God,** which is credited not only with numerous healings, but also with the salvation of Pskov from the troops of Stefan Batory in 1581 (2) (Fig. 2.16).

Fig. 2.14. St. Paphnutius Borovsky Monastery (3)

---

[1] Metropolitan Makarii (Bulgakov). History of the Russian Church. St. Petersburg, 1857.

[2] Icon of the Dormition of the Mother of God. URL: https://pskovo-pechersky-monastery.ru/icon/25-obraz-uspeniya-bozhiej-materi/ (accessed: 01.05.2021).

[3] St. Paphnutius Borovsky Monastery. URL: http://www.pafnuty-abbey.ru/ about/

Fig. 2.15. Holy Dormition Pskov-Pechersk Monastery

The image **of Joseph Volotsky**, who founded **the Volokolamsk Monastery** in 1479, was controversial (Fig. 2.17). He was a good manager of the monastery's property and, in the political disputes at the turn of the 15th and 16th centuries, became the head of an orthodox church group that demanded the unconditional blood of those he considered heretics. Meanwhile, his main opponent was **Nil Sorsky** (1433–1508), the author of "The Charter of Skete Life." Brother of Moscow deacon Andrei Maiko, Nil took monastic vows at the Kirillo-Belozersky Monastery, from which he set out in the mid-1470s on a pilgrimage to Byzantium, destroyed by the Turks, and to Mount Athos. Upon his return sometime in the early to mid-1480s, he founded a skete on the Sora River (Fig. 2.18).

"For Neil Sorsky, the concept of 'non-possession' is consistently used as a complete rejection of any kind of property (and even the desire to possess it) by a person who has taken a **monastic vow.**" (1) In turn, his main opponent, Joseph Volotsky, was firmly convinced that monasteries had the right to own land and exploit the labor of peasants. The Church was obliged to take care of the accumulation of wealth, which was used for its needs — primarily for

---

[1] Romanenko, E. V. Nil Sorsky and the Traditions of Russian Monasticism. Moscow: Pamjatniki Istoricheskoy Mysl, 2003. 255 p.

Fig. 2.16. Pskov-Pechersk Icon of the Dormition of the Mother of God

Fig. 2.17. Joseph Volotsky

Fig. 2.18. Neil Sorsky icon, 1908 (painted for the 400th anniversary of the death of the reverend)

Fig. 2.19. Joseph-Volotsky Monastery

church utensils and the maintenance of the monastic brotherhood. In addition, the need to give alms was one of the weighty arguments in the hands of Joseph and his followers in justifying the legitimacy of the monastery's policy of **acquisitiveness**" (1). (Figs. 2.19, 2.20).

---

[1] Zolotukhina N. M. Joseph of Volotsk. Moscow, 1981. pp. 46, 47.

Fig. 2.20. Monument to Joseph of Volotsk

However, there is another interpretation of the dispute between the "acquisitive" and the "non-acquisitive," which first arose in public at the Church Council of 1503. According to this point of view, the initiator of the issue of church land ownership was not the clergy, but Grand Duke Ivan III, who was in dire need of land grants for his nobility. As for Nil Sorsky, he should not be credited with a "categorical desire to introduce exclusively his own skete model of monastic life into the Russian Church"... The Reverend Nil "considered it possible to accept into his skete only those monks who had already passed the initial stage in communal monasteries," and nowhere in his writings did he "deny monastic land ownership as a whole." (1)

The disputes between the "acquisitive" and "non-acquisitive" took place at the turn of the 15th and 16th centuries, at a time when Moscow was becoming the undisputed capital of the centralized Russian state and its Kremlin was adorned with monumental stone cathedrals symbolizing the power of a rapidly growing country.

The Assumption Cathedral, built by Aristotle Fioravanti, became the temple where tsars were crowned, and **the Archangel Cathedral**, the creation of Alevisio Novi, became the burial place of the grand dukes. **The Cathedral of the Annunciation**, the house church of the sovereigns, and **the Cathedral of the Deposition of the Robe,** which served as the house church of the Moscow metropolitans, were also erected on Cathedral Square in the Kremlin (Figs. 2.21, 2.22).

However, holy places for Russians are not concentrated only in the capital. In the first quarter of the 15th century, local shepherds found one of

---

[1] Petrusko V. I. Moscow Cathedral 1503 // Vestnik PSTGU Series History. History of the Russian Orthodox Church. 2016.№ 6. P. 15.

Fig. 2.21. Assumption Cathedral of the Moscow Kremlin

Fig. 2.22. Archangel Cathedral of the Moscow Kremlin

the most famous miraculous crosses, with stylistic Byzantine roots. A wooden church was built on this site, which was rebuilt after a fire and replaced by a stone church in the 18th century. Currently, **the Life-Giving Cross of the Lord** is located in the village of Gedenovo in the Ivanovo Region in **the Church of John Chrysostom,** and on holidays it is visited by up to 10,000 pilgrims (Fig. 2.23, 2.24).

Fig. 2.23. Church of John Chrysostom in Godenovo

Fig. 2.24. The Godenovo Cross

Church councils became an important manifestation of public life in Muscovy, which, in the context of the formation of a centralized state, went beyond narrow confessional issues. This was particularly true of **the Stoglav Council of 1551**, whose sessions lasted several months. **Metropolitan Makarii** presided over the council, and its participants included nine archbishops (Tver, Smolensk, Ryazan, Perm, Rostov, Krutitsy, Suzdal, Novgorod, and Kolomna), bishops, archimandrites, abbots, and boyars. Opening the council, Tsar Ivan IV handed over a number of texts with questions, which the participants attempted to answer in the final document. The structure of the latter is "very vague and difficult to fully comprehend." "The answers sometimes stray from the topics outlined in the 'questions' (1). This apparently testifies to the fierce struggle that unfolded at the Council, which ultimately ended in a compromise between the secular and spiritual authorities. Most likely, "in financial terms, the bishops achieved the best results for themselves, while the monasteries had the hardest time... At the same time, the decisions of the main part of the Stoglav do not reduce the expenses of the state treasury" (2).

The Council systematized all the norms of existing church law. In particular, it resolved issues such as the establishment of the size of bishop's duties, the powers of the ecclesiastical court, the state of discipline among the clergy, and the care of the poor. The principle of complete independence of the church in its affairs was legalized.

At the same time, a reasonable limit was set on the further growth of church land ownership. In particular, the "Verdict on Estates" emphasized the prohibition on acquiring land without the tsar's permission through purchase or donation and engaging in usury.

The council "abolished monetary grants ("ruga") from the tsar's treasury to those monasteries that had significant land holdings.

...The sovereign took possession of those monastic lands which, during the boyar rule preceding the accession of Ivan IV, had been transferred to the monasteries. The infringement of the church's property rights continued thereafter. "At the Council of 1572, the wealthy monks were prohibited from acquiring land through gifts from private individuals, and in 1580 — through

---

[1] Cherepnin, L. V. Zemsky Councils of the Russian State in the 16th–17th Centuries. Moscow, 1978. P. 81.

[2] Shaposhnik V. V. Financial Issues at the Stoglav Council // Christian Reading. 2014. No. 1 pp. 112, 111.

wills, deeds of sale, and mortgage deeds. The Council of 1584 equated the church as a legal entity with a private individual and directly made it dependent on the will of the state. (1)

XVI c. — This was a time not only of consolidation of Russian lands, but also of Orthodoxy and active church construction. "According to the calculations of Ya. E. Volodarsky, 154 monasteries were founded in the 9th– 13th centuries, another 145 in the 14th century, 205 in the 15th century, and 409 in the 16th century. By the end of the 16th century, there should have been 754–771 monasteries, but some of the monasteries that had been built earlier ceased to exist. According to another version based on data from V. V. Zverinsky and written sources, from 988 to 1240 there were presumably 116 monasteries, between 1240 and 1448, another 286 were established, and between 1448 and the end of the 16th century, 486 new monasteries appeared (2). However, in reality there were more, since the centers of monastic life in the western dioceses, which were not subordinate to Moscow at that time, are not taken into account.

One of the most remarkable events was the founding of **the Nil-Stolobensky Monastery** on Lake Seliger near the town of Ostashkov at the end of the 16th century. The monastery was opened in honor of the hermit Nil, who lived in this amazing place for 27 years and was loved by the local residents. Until the beginning of the 20th century, the monastery was one of the most revered in Russia — thousands of people came here every year, and the number of permanent residents reached 1 000.

***

At the end of the 16th century, a significant event took place in the life of Russian Orthodoxy — Moscow succeeded in establishing a patriarchate. And although "given the current state of sources, it is impossible to definitively determine the main author of the idea of establishing a patriarchal throne in Moscow" (3) — Tsar Feodor Ivanovich, the powerful brother of his wife Boris Godunov, the opposition boyars Shuisky or Metropolitan Dionysius, the main thing is that the Muscovite kingdom managed to sharply raise its international prestige.

---

[1] Chernukha V. V., Timoshenko G. A. Economic and political-legal aspects of church and monastic land ownership in the history of Russia // News of the Orenburg State Agrarian University. 2016. No. 2. P. 244.

[2] Kolycheva E. M. Orthodox monasteries in the second half of the 15th century // Monasticism and monasteries in Russia... P. 86.

[3] Volodikhin, D. M. Metropolitan Dionysius Grammaticus of Moscow and All Russia as the Presumed Author of the Idea of Establishing a Patriarchal See in Moscow // Historical Review. 2019.№ 2. P. 28–44.

"The importance of the Russian hierarchy also grew... Previously, church hierarchs were not always invited to the Zemsky Sobors. Now, however, the hierarchy has become mandatory permanent members of the Zemsky Sobors." (1). The establishment of the patriarchate was followed by internal organizational changes: the former archbishops (Novgorod, Kazan, Rostov, Krutitsy) were elevated to the rank of metropolitans. Clergymen in Vologda, Suzdal, Smolensk, Ryazan, and Tver became archbishops.

***

An important feature of Russian social life, which apparently did not fade away over time but only grew stronger, was **collectivism**. This collectivism was determined primarily by the difficult natural and climatic conditions, with an unusually short working season for agriculture, which required the greatest concentration of labor in a short period of time and was compensated for by the enormous role of the peasant community. At the same time, the peasant community became a stronghold of local solidarity and a means of peasant resistance (2).

The most active, rebellious members of the community fled to the outskirts of the state, as this was possible, unlike in overpopulated Western Europe. "Taking advantage of the government's lack of attention to the outskirts, thousands of peasants fled to the Don, the Kuban and Caucasus regions, the Lower Volga region, the Urals, and to a lesser extent to Siberia and the Far East, hoping to find freedom in the vast uninhabited lands"(3). In particular, "the south and southeast of Russia experienced a period of strong economic revival in the second half of the 16th century."

In the Tula district, over a short period of time — from 1585 to 1588/89 — the area of cultivated land more than doubled... In the Oryol district, as a result of 30 years of colonization, by 1594/95 there were 1 337 peasant and 91 bobyl households," "only about 1/6 of the available area suitable for

---

[1] Archimandrite Makarii (Veretennikov). The First Patriarch Job and His Time // Bulletin of the Yekaterinburg Theological Seminary. 2018.№ 1. P. 65.

[2] Milov L. V. The Great Russian Plowman and the Peculiarities of the Russian Historical Process. Moscow: ROSPEN, 1998.

[3] Koretsky V. I. The Formation of Serfdom and the First Peasant War in Russia. Moscow, 1975. pp. 83, 85.

cultivation was plowed for land cultivation" (1). Here, collectivist principles were reproduced in a new environment, free from serfdom, in the form **of the Cossacks**. Of course, the composition of the Cossacks was more complex than just fugitive peasants from Central Russia. In the 16th–17th centuries "Cossacks were called robbers of Ukraine, Tatars in Russian service, homeless workers, runaway slaves, wanderers; in the steppe, the Cossacks implied freedom and self-will, with some Cossacks being called "thieves" and others "servants," but in reality their roles alternated" (2).

Cossacks, whose origins are linked to the mixing of Slavs and Turks on the steppe borderlands during the collapse of the Golden Horde and the creation of Russian-Turkic communities of a semi-military, semi-criminal nature (3), later, as serfdom became established, had runaway peasants as their source of replenishment. "Peasants, archers, and warriors went alone and in groups, mostly joining the Cossack embassies returning from Moscow. Often the atamans themselves... persuaded the Muscovites to go with them to the Don" (4). Apparently, their numbers increased during the years of crop failure (1601–1603) and during the Time of Troubles, but after it ended, the government was quite passive in returning the fugitives (5).

The spirit of collectivist rebellion was fully manifested in the Peasant Wars of the 17th–18th centuries, which arose on the outskirts of the state and then attempted to spread to the central regions. The core of this rebellious movement was made up of Cossacks (among whom social differentiation was taking place) and the disenfranchised foreign population that joined them. (6)

---

[1] Kolomeitseva, M. A. Stages of the Formation of the Peasant Class on the Don in the 17th–First Half of the 19th Centuries // Bulletin of the Institute for Comprehensive Research on Agrarian Territories. 2010.№ 2 (21). P. 131.

[2] Golovnev A. V. The Living Border: Cossack Maneuvers in the Space of Colonization (turn of the 16th–17th centuries) // Tractus aevorum, Research Institute of BelSU. 2015. P. 106.

[3] Medvedev, A. The True History of the Russian and Ukrainian Peoples. Moscow, 2015. pp. 83, 84.

[4] Savelyev, E. P. The Peasant Question in the Don Region in Connection with the Cossacks. Historical and Statistical Essay. Novocherkassk, 1917. pp. 17–18.

[5] Lyapin, D. A. Cases involving peasants in southern Russia in the 1620s // Bulletin of Volgograd University. Series 4. History. Regional Studies. International Relations. 2020. Vol. 25,№ 5. P. 165.

[6] Sopov A. V. The Origin of the Cossacks: Returning to the Problem // Bulletin of Moscow University. Series 8. History. 2011.№ 1. P. 61, 62.

The First Peasant War of 1606–1607, led by **Ivan Bolotnikov,** was particularly dangerous for the state, as it took place during a period of "interregnum." The leader himself began his venture as an emissary of one of the impostors, "Tsarevich Peter," and his troops included many nobles. In **the Second Peasant War** of 1667–1671, led by **S. Razin,** "along with serfs as the main force of the movement... plebeian elements of the city, workers in crafts and water transport... took part (more than before)," as well as the Don Cossacks. During the uprising led **by K. Bulavin** (1706–1797), which was based in the Don region, the participants included the same Cossacks, runaway peasants, soldiers, and townspeople, but a new element was added in the form of schismatics, Bashkirs, and Tatars. The peasant war, **led by E. Pugachev** in 1773–1775**,** turned out to be the most organized, involving workers from Ural factories and peasants assigned to the factories, who supplied the rebels with weapons and ammunition. "There were regiments consisting of different peoples (Bashkirs, Kalmyks), Cossacks (Iset, Yaik, Iletsk), factory peasants, etc." (1).

It is characteristic that after the 1770s, mass social movements of this level were no longer observed in Russia, which can be explained by several circumstances: the increased effectiveness of the government's repressive policies and control over the periphery, and a decrease in the level of exploitation of the population. Nevertheless, the memory of the peasant wars remained in folklore, and the rebellious spirit was preserved in the population at a genetic level, which clearly manifested itself in the years of the revolutions of the early 20th century.

Another manifestation of Russian collectivism is **the collectivism of unity**, which is socially encouraged by the authorities. Zemsky Sobors, or "assemblies of the whole land," grew out of church or zemsky-church assemblies (the latter also invited secular Figures in the form of the boyars). "... The zemsky sobory were intended to serve as an external expression of the political unification of Great Russia under the single authority of the Moscow tsar and to unite the small zemsky worlds that had remained divided since the times of the appanage system. In addition, this new body was intended to serve as a support for the strengthened autocratic power of the Moscow tsars

---

[1] Cherepnin, L. V. Introduction. On the study of peasant wars in Russia in the 17th–18th centuries: gaps, searches, solutions. Moscow, 1974. pp. 13, 16, 17.

in their dispute with the boyars..." (1). He performed information and communication functions for the authorities. At the same time, "at the Council, society was represented not by elected representatives, but by officials whose powers, however, could be based both on administrative appointment and on public election" (2). The first Zemsky Sobor was held in 1550, and then these meetings in the 1550s and 1560s were devoted to military and judicial issues.

One might assume that the councils served some internal purpose of Ivan IV's reign, who fought resolutely against the feudal nobility. But no. They were also held under subsequent rulers, and their significance did not diminish, but only increased. The council of 1584 was devoted to the confirmation of Ivan IV's son Fyodor as tsar, and the council of 1598 to the election of Boris Godunov as tsar in connection with the suppression of the Rurik dynasty.

Historians interpret this dramatic event in Russian history in different ways. I. D. Belyaev, N. P. Zagoskin, and V. N. Latkin see it as clear manipulation on the part of Boris Godunov's supporters; S. M. Solovyov, V. O. Klyuchevsky, and M. N. Tikhomirov see no predetermination or malicious intent in what happened (3). At the same time, the number and class composition of the participants is estimated by specific authors to be approximately 500–600 people. According to V. O. Klyuchevsky, there were 109 clergymen, 30 boyars, okolnichy, Duma nobles, and Duma clerks, 18 palace officials, 267 military personnel, 21 guests, and 15 elders of the guest, cloth, and black Moscow hundreds. S. P. Mordovina provides slightly different information: almost all members of the Boyar Duma (38 people), most of the Moscow nobles (104), all stolniks (25), etc (4) In other words, secular and spiritual feudal lords, as well as the upper echelons of the posad population, took part in the electoral process.

It is natural that during **the Time of Troubles, the factor of collective meetings of "the whole land" increased sharply**. Moreover, these bodies,

---

[1] Kudryavtsev, M. A. V. O. Klyuchevsky's views on the Zemsky Sobors. The ratio of administrative and representative elements in their activities // Proceedings of the Institute of State and Law of the Russian Academy of Sciences. 2015.№ 5. P. 150.

[2] Ibid. p. 151.

[3] Cherepnin, L. V. Zemsky Sobors of the Russian State in the 16th–17th Centuries, Moscow, 1978. pp. 133–135.

[4] Ibid. pp. 145–146.

uniting nobles, townspeople, and peasants, arose locally, initially in the southeastern cities (1).

During a period of acute internal political crisis, clashes between pretenders to the throne, the boyar tsar V. Shuisky, and Polish interventionists, "zemstvo institutions were used by opposing political parties as a tool in the struggle for power." There was a revival of zemstvo activity, which found expression in the organization of posad communities (2).

At the final stage of the Time of Troubles, when the threat to Russian statehood reached a critical point, city councils, which included local church hierarchs (who often headed these councils), townspeople, and servicemen, began to perform the function of patriotic mobilization. They were the ones who set about creating local militias and resisting False Dmitry II and the Polish invaders. "In February 1611, zemsky militias from Vladimir, Nizhny Novgorod, Murom, Yaroslavl, Pereslavl-Zalessky, Uglich, Suzdal, Vologda, Galich, Kostroma, and Romanov (Romanov-Borisoglebsk) marched on Moscow. Troops of Volga Cossacks and Cherkasy (Dnieper Cossacks) also marched there."(3) A "Council of the Whole Land" and a Zemsky government were established in a camp near Moscow. However, the second militia, which was formed on the initiative of Nizhny Novgorod, proved to be more organized and successful. A new "Council of the Whole Land" was created in Yaroslavl, to which "the people of Nizhny Novgorod called on Russian cities to send 'two men from every people'". Orders were organized. "At the same time, voivodes were appointed from Yaroslavl to Ustyuzhna, Beloozero, Vladimir, Kasimov, Klin, Tver, Kostroma, Rostov, Suzdal, Pereslavl, Tobolsk and other cities of the Moscow State." (4)

The best illustration of Russian unity is **the Zemsky Sobor of 1613**, convened after the expulsion of Polish invaders from Moscow. Assessing this assembly of elected representatives from the regions realistically

---

[1] Nazarov V. D., Florya B. N. The peasant uprising led by I. I. Bolotnikov and the Polish-Lithuanian Commonwealth // Peasant wars in Russia in the 17th–18th centuries. Moscow, 1974. P. 351.

[2] Arakcheev V. A. Zemsky Mir and the Zemsky Movement in Russia during the Time of Troubles (1606–1616) // News of the A. I. Herzen State Pedagogical University. 2008.№ 48. P. 27–34.

[3] Perevozentsov, S. V. Traditions of Popular Rule in Russia in the 15th–17th Centuries // Bulletin of Moscow University. Series 12. Political Sciences. 2017.№ 3. P. 55.

[4] Ibid. pp. 59, 60.

(i.e., noting the absence of representation of all classes and acute political struggle), nevertheless, one cannot fail to recognize its broad social composition. "Thus, it is documented that the Electoral Council consisted of 40 to 50 representatives of the clergy, 16 boyars and okolnichy, about 40 militia commanders, about 20 officials, about 20 city commanders, and approximately 300 electors from the cities. A total of almost 500 people" (1).

The election of the tsar was not without difficulties. Initially, one of the organizers of the First Militia, Boyar D. T. Trubetskoy, had the best chances. He was supported by prominent representatives of the clergy and young militia commanders, but not by the noble boyars. In February, when the boyars and representatives from the cities arrived at the council, the number of contenders for the throne increased, and the participants agreed on a compromise candidate, Tsar Fyodor Ivanovich's second cousin Mikhail Romanov (2).

In the future, the young, fragile government was forced to resort to convening councils every year (until 1622). "In 1614, the Zemsky Sobor sent an embassy of clergy and secular Figures to persuade the Cossacks to renounce their 'thievery'. In 1614–1617, the Zemsky Sobor was engaged in organizing the financial support of the state... In September 1616, the council considered the question of concluding peace with Switzerland. In 1619, the Zemsky Sobor was devoted to "organizing" and "correcting the land" (3).

From 1632, the Zemsky Sobors resumed their activities, and some of them, such as the Sobor of 1648–1649, which drafted the Sobornoye Ulozheniye of 1649, had a decisive impact on the sphere of state administration. Nevertheless, the importance of this collective body, which clearly resembled a medieval European parliament, declined more and more.

V. O. Klyuchevsky is right in asserting that "popular representation arose in our country not to limit power, but to find and strengthen it: this is how it differs from Western European representation" (4). Although "there are parallels to the Zemsky Sobors in England (parliament), France and the Netherlands (States General), Germany (Reichstag, Landtags), Scandinavia (Riksdag), and the Czech Republic and Poland (Sejm)"(5), the conditions of social development in Russia fundamentally different from Western Europe,

---

[1] Morozova, L. E. History of Russia. The Time of Troubles. Truth and Fiction in Contemporary Accounts. Moscow, 2011. p. 516.

[2] Ibid. pp. 515, 520.

[3] Perevezentsev, S. V. Traditions of Democracy in Russia... p. 61.

[4] Klyuchevsky, V. O. Works: in 9 vols. Vol. 3. Moscow, 1988. pp. 197, 198.

[5] Cherepnin, L. V. Zemsky Sobors of the Russian State... p. 397.

which inevitably had an impact on Russian institutions. First, "the class system in Russia was characterized by... relatively great diversity..." Second, "the predominantly agrarian nature of the country and the weakness of Russian cities and urban structures limited the role of the 'third estate' in political life. (1) Muscovy simply did not need a body to satisfy petty particular interests: it needed something greater and more important — the achievement of social harmony, especially in times of crisis in its history.

***

After the start of imperial construction in the mid-16th century, spiritual and religious education of **the** new **eastern territories** and the local population became an important priority. Immediately after the capture of Kazan, Orthodox churches were built in the city — **the Church of the Savior Not Made by Hands, the Church of Cyprian and Justina, the Annunciation Cathedral, and the Zilant Monastery** outside the city. Over time, **the Trinity-Sergius** and **Dormition monasteries** were established **in Sviyazhsk** (Fig. 2.25).

Fig. 2.25. Sviyazhsk Monastery of the Dormition

---

[1] Cherepnin L. V. Zemsky Sobors of the Russian State... pp. 398, 399.

The Tatar population converted to Orthodox Christianity in whole families. Two Kazan kings were baptized in Moscow, followed by Tatar nobles. Efforts were made to settle Kazan with Russians, and in 1555 a new diocese was opened there.

Archbishop **Saint Guriy**, elected at the Moscow Council, received from the tsar and the metropolitan "Instruction" from the tsar and the metropolitan, which prescribed converting the local Tatar population to Orthodoxy not through fear, but through love. It was necessary to protect people from possible arbitrariness on the part of the secular authorities.

Efforts to spread the Christian faith were also undertaken in the southeastern government.

Fig. 2.26. Archbishop Cyprian. Illustration from the book "Lights of Siberia"

Although no separate bishopric was established in Astrakhan, **a monastery dedicated to the Holy Trinity and St. Nicholas** was founded. The Circassian princes, who turned to Moscow for protection from Crimea, also became Christians, as did the Kabardians.

Orthodox Christianity arrived in Siberia at the end of the 16th century. In 1586, **the first Russian city, Tyumen**, was founded, along with **churches dedicated to St. Nicholas and the Nativity of the Blessed Virgin Mary. The first Archbishop of Tobolsk, Cyprian** (1620–1624), founded several monasteries and churches and put an end to the tyranny of the Siberian governor (Fig. 2.26). By the time of his departure, there were 30 churches, 12 monasteries, 300 clergymen, and 50 monks and nuns in Siberia. However, the head of the Siberian See, **Philotheus** (1702–1711 and 1715–1725), is considered the true Apostle of Siberia. It was he who established a new school for bishops and sent missionaries to Kamchatka. He also developed his own active missionary work in the Ob and Irtysh river basins, which required considerable courage in view of the resistance of the pagan nobility. Later, during a two-year tour of his vast diocese, he visited the cities of Tomsk, Turukhansk, Yeniseysk, and Irkutsk.

Fig. 2.27. Metropolitan Philotheus of Siberia and Tobolsk

He was baptized the Yenisei Ostiaks, Chulym Tatars, and Kistimtsy, and sowed the first seeds of Christianity among the Tungus and Kamchadals. According to the calculations of his successor, Philotheus baptized up to 40,000 foreigners and built 37 churches among them (1) (Fig. 2.27).

The western and southern lands of Russia, which came under the control of the Polish-Lithuanian Commonwealth, unfortunately experienced religious oppression and humiliation at the hands of the Catholic Church. At that time, Russia was unable to help them in any way. Religious intolerance intensified with the arrival of the Jesuits in 1576. Not only did they bring back to the Catholic Church those who had left (2), but also imposed a union on Orthodoxy in 1595.

Uniatism had partial success: the Russian-Lithuanian nobility turned away from Orthodoxy, but the common people remained loyal to it. The price for this was persecution of the steadfast on the basis of inspired denunciations. As a deputy from the Volhynia region complained at the Warsaw Sejm, "in the big cities, Orthodox churches have long been sealed, church estates cleared, and livestock locked up in monasteries." In Pinsk, "the Leshchinsky monastery has been turned into a drinking house; unbaptized children are being taken away from this world, and the bodies of the dead are being carried out of the cities without a church ceremony..." (3).

The situation was partially rectified during the reign of King Vladislav IV, who was approached at the time of his enthronement by Archimandrite **Peter Mogila** (1596–1647) of the Kiev-Pechersk Lavra, the future Metropolitan of Kiev, Galicia, and All Rus'. The king recognized four Orthodox dioceses and metropolitans for the first time, despite the discontent

---

[1] Efimov, A. B. Essays on the History of Missionary Work of the Russian Orthodox Church. Moscow: PSTGU Publishing House, 2007. 688 p.

[2] History of the Southern and Western Slavs. Vol. 1. The Middle Ages and Modern Times / ed. by G. F. Matveev and Z. S. Nenasheva. Moscow, 2008. pp. 234–236.

[3] Bryantsev, P. The Lithuanian State... pp. 434–435.

of the Catholic and Uniate clergy. The free practice of Orthodox Christianity was permitted, as was the restoration and construction of new churches and the creation of brotherhoods, schools, seminaries, and printing houses. After the merger of the two schools, **the Kiev-Mohyla Academy** was established—the first institution of higher education in the East Slavic lands (renamed the Academy in 1701).

However, Petro Mohyla's activities have always raised many questions and ambiguous interpretations: on the one hand, he socially legalized Orthodox Christianity in Ukraine and Belarus, but on the other hand, many of his innovations are seen as the result of the influence of the Roman Catholic Church and Western culture" (Fig. 2.28). and Western culture" (Fig. 2.28).

Fig. 2.28. Metropolitan of Kiev, Galicia, and All Rus' Peter Mohyla

***

XVII was marked not only by the spread of Orthodoxy as the empire grew, but also by the emergence of acute intra-confessional strife. **Patriarch Nikon,** the favorite of the young Tsar Alexei Fedorovich, played a very controversial role in this. He was elevated to the ranks of the church hierarchy by a circle of "zealots of piety" popular at court. This group, concerned about the insufficient morality and piety of the clergy, advocated for church reforms. It was led by the archpriest of the Annunciation Cathedral in the Kremlin, the tsar's confessor and mentor, Stefan Vonifatyev, boyar F. M. Rtishchev, and archpriest of the Kazan Cathedral, Ioann Mironov. Nikon, a peasant from the Nizhny Novgorod region, joined the circle of reformers after becoming archimandrite **of the Novospassky Monastery**, a monastery that enjoyed the special favor of the first tsars of the Romanov dynasty (Fig. 2.29).

Fig. 2.29. Patriarch Nikon.
Portrait of the patriarch, 1660–1665.

His new position gave Nikon the opportunity to visit Alexei Mikhailovich at the palace every Friday for conversations and advice. In 1649, this proximity allowed Nikon to become Metropolitan of Novgorod and demonstrate his strict administrative nature. He acted in accordance with the program of the "zealots of piety": he demanded that priests deliver sermons in full, rather than in abridged form, insisted that rituals be performed in accordance with Greek traditions, and arranged for bread to be distributed to the poor and hungry. After the death of Patriarch Joseph (1642–1652), Nikon was elevated to the patriarchal rank.

However, fundamental differences soon emerged between ordinary, provincial "zealots of piety," who came into conflict with their parishioners because of the "strictness" of their preaching "strictness" they preached, and the new patriarch. "While simple provincial "priests" zealously denounced the vices and weaknesses of their parishioners, receiving only insults and beatings in response, in Moscow, at court, church affairs were viewed much more broadly. The government of Alexei Mikhailovich was inclined to believe in the need to revise all church rites and bring them into line with Greek liturgical practice." (1).

The motives for these reforms apparently lay not in the establishment of absolutism, as claimed in Soviet historiography, but in foreign policy: the Russian state needed to strengthen its international prestige in connection with the annexation of Ukraine. Nikon, acting passionately and impatiently, "wanted to raise the prestige of the Moscow Patriarchate in the Orthodox world" (2). As for the conflict among the clergy, initially in 1653, it was personal in nature between the "zealots of piety" and the patriarch, touching on issues of corporate discipline, and later, from 1654, after the publication of recommendations on innovations in worship, it began to take on an ideological dimension.

The main innovations in the rites were the prohibition of kneeling bows (i.e., only waist bows were allowed) and the permission to make the sign of the cross only with three fingers, not two. Corrections were made to the liturgical books based on Greek models, but all this was done hastily and without a system. At the same time, "the first measures to change church rites according to the Greek model did not cause widespread protest, but rather passive rejection or indifference."

"The turning point, from which the flight into schism took on a mass character, should be considered the church council with the participation of Greek hierarchs in 1667 (3).

By that time, Patriarch Nikon had demonstratively left the patriarchal see in the summer of 1658 and gone to the New Jerusalem Resurrection Monastery. The rift between the tsar and the patriarch could have been smoothed over at an early stage, but the power-hungry church hierarch sought to realize his ambitious claims to power: in **particular, the repeal of provisions of the 1649 Judicial Code that were inconvenient for the church and** imposed property and judicial restrictions on church organization.

---

[1] Borisov, N. S. Church Figures of medieval Russia in the 13th–18th centuries. Moscow: Moscow State University, 1988. P. 176.

[2] Vernadsky G. The Moscow Kingdom. Moscow, 2017. P. 305.

[3] Lobachev, S. V. Patriarch Nikon. St. Petersburg, 2003. pp. 12, 26.

At some point, "Nikon finally realized what a big mistake he had made by leaving the capital, overestimating his influence on the tsar. The tone of his letters to the autocrat changed: from humbly Christian to capriciously demanding, then to humbly passionate. As a result, he decided on an extreme measure: contrary to his previous statements, Nikon declared that although he had left Moscow of his own free will, he still considered himself patriarch, had "grace" upon him, and could perform **healings**." (1).

The Moscow authorities found themselves in a difficult situation. For a long time, they did not dare to launch a direct attack. Meanwhile, Nikon's theocratic statements became increasingly frank. Clearly disregarding the Byzantine concept of the "symphony of powers" and the established Byzantine practice of imperial responsibility for church affairs (2), the hierarch who had left the capital stated that the priesthood was above the kingdom.

An attempt to depose Nikon at the church council in 1660 was met with resistance from Epiphanius Slavinetsky, an expert on canonical rules. Later, the former bishop of the Jerusalem Church, Paisius Ligari, took it upon himself to organize the condemnation of Nikon, relying on the authority of the Eastern patriarchs. However, the patriarchs were in no hurry to arrive — moreover, the patriarchs of Constantinople and Jerusalem refused to come to Moscow.

The Great Council of 1666–1667, which condemned Nikon, took place in two stages. Initially, from February to June 1666, Russian hierarchs certified the conformity of the activities of the Greek patriarchs and Greek liturgical books with Orthodoxy and condemned the opponents of church reform. In the second stage, which began on November 28, 1666, when the patriarchs of Alexandria and Antioch arrived in Moscow, Nikon was deposed from the patriarchal office and the archimandrite of the Trinity-Sergius Monastery was elected in his place. As a result, a number of resolutions of the Stoglav Council of 1551 that opposed church reform were rejected, and church rules of an organizational, ritual, iconographic, and behavioral nature were revised. The names of the bishoprics were distributed among the cities in the composition of 5 metropolises, 6 archbishoprics, and 8 bishoprics under the authority of the patriarch, and the creation of new dioceses was recommended.

---

[1] Borisov N. S. Church Figures of medieval Rus... p. 188.

[2] Velichko, A. M. The Church and the Emperor in Byzantine and Russian History (Historical and Legal Essays). St. Petersburg, 2006. pp. 12–50.

The Great Council did not lead to reconciliation, but rather to a deepening of the schism in the Russian Orthodox Church. The condemnation of its leaders, Archpriest Avvakum Petrov, Priest Lazar, Deacon Fyodor, and others, was followed by an uprising in the Solovetsky Monastery (1667–1671) and the execution of 28 monks. In the first half of the 1670s, boyarina Feodosia Morozova and her sister Evdokia Urusova, as well as the wife of Streltsy colonel Maria Danilova, suffered persecution by the Moscow authorities. The Local Council of 1681 asked the tsar to intensify repression against the zealots of the old ways, resulting in the mass execution of Old Believers in 1682.

Meanwhile, despite repression, which weakened during the 18th and 19th centuries, the latter constituted up to a third of the population. According to other estimates by P. I. Melnikov-Pechersky, between 12 and 14 million people adhered to Old Belief in the second half of the 19th century, i.e., approximately one-fifth of Russian Christians (1). In one way or another, the deposed Patriarch Nikon, and with him the autocracy, made a gross socio-political and religious mistake, opposing the reforms with a huge mass of the population that was not ready to accept them. However, Nikon did have some merits before Russian society: it was on his initiative that two famous monasteries were built. **The Resurrection New Jerusalem Monastery** in the city of Istra was founded in 1656 with the aim of recreating the complex of holy places in Palestine. The Resurrection Cathedral was built in the image and likeness of the Church of the Holy Sepulchre. The library collected by the patriarch was of great value, including Greek manuscripts from the Athonite monasteries with texts by ancient and early Christian authors, books published in Western and Southern Rus (Fig. 2.30).

In 1653, a proposal was made to establish a monastery similar to the Iveron Monastery on Mount Athos. Two temporary wooden churches were erected on the island on Lake Valdai, and parts of the relics of Saints Peter, Jonah, and Philip were brought from Moscow. Meanwhile, in 1655, a second copy (the first was delivered in 1648) of the miraculous Iveron Icon arrived in Moscow from Mount Athos, and in December 1665, it took its place in the monastery on Valdai (Fig. 2 .31). In memory of the salvation from the cholera epidemic in 1848, Emperor Nicholas I approved the decision of His Holiness

---

[1] Fedorov V. A. The Orthodox Church and the State / Essays on Russian Culture of the 19th Century / Ed. by L. V. Koshman. Vol. 2. Moscow, 2000. P. 305.

Fig. 2.30. New Jerusalem Monastery in the city of Istra

Synod on the establishment of the Cross Procession with the miraculous icon from **the Iversky Monastery, held** annually on July 28 around the city of Valdai (1) (Fig. 2.32).

***

Summarizing the spiritual state of Russian society and statehood at the end of the 17th century, it should be noted that the acceptability of grand ducal power logically and naturally transformed into **adherence to autocracy** during the mid-16th to 17th centuries (Diagram 2.1). The Orthodox faith in the minds of Russians was strengthened in the form of "adherence to tradition" and the rejection of any compromise with Catholicism. The relative independence of the church during the period of Tatar-Mongol rule and the weakening of princely power were corrected with the beginning of the construction of a centralized Russian state and the implementation of a healthy "symphony of powers."

This was also facilitated by the concept that inspired Russians, namely that after the fall of Constantinople in 1453, Moscow became the "Third Rome," i.e., essentially a model for all others Orthodox churches.

---

[1] Iversky Monastery in Valdai. URL: https://iveron.ru/ iverskaya-ikona-bozhiej-materi/ (accessed: 21.06.2019).

Fig. 2.31. Iversky Cathedral: Icon of the Mother of God of Iveron

Fig. 2.32. Valdai Iversky Monastery

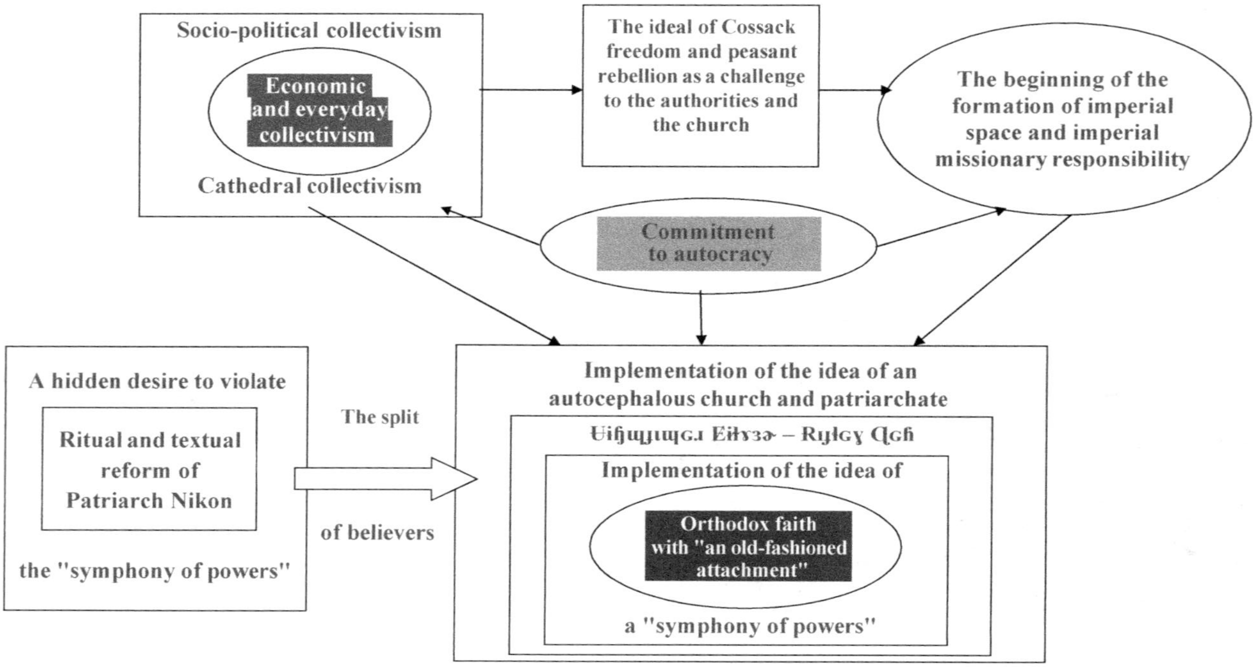

Diagram 2.1. Concept Moscow – Third Rome

In accordance with this concept, at the end of the 16th century, the Moscow authorities added the establishment of a patriarchate to genuine autocephaly.

Another important component of the spiritual core of Muscovy was collectivism — initially in its economic and everyday expression (thanks to the stability of the peasant community), and then, from the middle of the 16th century, in its socio-political (conciliar) form.

A well-known distortion of this collectivity was the ideal of rebellion and freedom, realized by fugitive peasants on the outskirts of the state and the Cossacks who formed there. This rebellious collectivism, which reached its peak during the periods of mass peasant wars in the 17th and 18th centuries, posed a well-known danger to the state. At the same time, it contributed to the more rapid development of the state's outskirts and the institutionalization of the imperial space. Let us not forget that the main territorial expansion of our Fatherland took place precisely before the end of the 17th century. The spiritual integration of these new territories was facilitated by the missionary activity of Orthodox clergy.

However, despite all the positive developments in Muscovy in the second half of the 17th century, a serious administrative mistake was made, which in the future threatened to complicate matters for the state and society. Patriarch Nikon's hasty and authoritarian ritual and textual church reform, apparently largely motivated by his personal ambitions for power, divided believers and prompted the secular authorities to establish stricter control over the church. Unfortunately, this disrupted the optimal balance between the secular and spiritual spheres and made Russians more susceptible to social emotions.

Essay 3
STAGED SECULARIZATION OF THE SPIRITUAL COLLECTIVIST CODE IN THE RUSSIAN EMPIRE, 18TH — EARLY 20TH CENTURY

The general trend at the end of the European Middle Ages (i.e., in the 16th–17th centuries) was **a decline in religious monopoly and religious fanaticism**. This was most evident in the Reformation in European countries, when Catholicism was challenged by various Protestant movements. On the other hand, there were also attempts at religious synthesis, such as in the Mughal Empire in India by Shah Akbar (1556–1605) (1).

The secularization of public consciousness, expressed in a decline in its religious dominance, was closely linked to the secularization of the economy (i.e., the confiscation of church property by the state). Partial, selective secularization of property had been attempted before, for example, from time to time in Byzantium, which found itself in a difficult geopolitical and domestic political situation in the 7th–8th centuries. Even in the West, where the church claimed independent political power in times of danger, Charles Martel in the 8th century sought to limit its property interests.

However, from the 17th–18th centuries in the West, and then in other countries, it is legitimate to speak of **comprehensive secularization**, not only **in terms of property**, but also **in terms of politics** (the weakening of the powers of church hierarchs), **the judiciary** (the expansion of secular jurisdiction), **education** (the elimination of the church's monopoly on education), **scientific and cultural** (loss of religious control over most of science and culture), **and worldview** (the emergence of a more secular, more rational picture of the universe) secularization (2).

---

[1] Vasilyev L. S. History of the East. Moscow, 1993. Vol. 1. P. 331.

[2] Secularization as a process and phenomenon — types, characteristics, significance. URL: https://velikayakultura.ru/fenomeny-sovramennoy-kultury/sekulyarizatsiay-kak-protses-u-fenomen-vidy-cherty-znachenie (accessed: 21.09.2021).

In Russia, these processes progressed at a slower pace than in Europe. To a certain extent, a political push from the highest secular authorities was required during **the Westernization** undertaken by Peter I.

The abolition of the patriarchate, apparently, in the context of Peter's reforms, was a necessary and inevitable measure on the part of the reformist tsar. However, this justified tactical decision, aimed at neutralizing social conservatism, proved to be unsuccessful in strategic terms and led to **the nationalization of the church** and a decline in its authority.

Initially, after the death of Patriarch Adrian in 1700, Peter I refused only to elect a full successor to him, and by decree of December 16, 1700, he established a temporary collegial administration of spiritual affairs. Bishop **Stefan Yavorsky** of Ryazan and Moscow, a representative of the Little Russian religious tradition, was appointed as **the temporary holder of the patriarchal throne**, but his powers were severely curtailed (Fig. 3.1). In particular, the administration of monasteries was entrusted to the Monastery Order headed by Musin-Pushkin. Certain rules were adopted for the proper functioning of monasteries, and the "surplus" of their property (about 6,500 peasant households) was transferred to the treasury and earmarked for the maintenance of almshouses.

Fig. 3.1. Bishop Stefan Yavorsky of Ryazan and Moscow

The creation of the Senate in 1711 dealt another blow to the autonomy of the church organization. "The deputy patriarch could no longer appoint a bishop to a diocese without the consent of the senators. If he tried to intervene in disputes... he was cut off, and he left the meeting in tears" (1). In the end, S. Yavorsky, as it turned out, was not at all the Figure that the reforming tsar needed. He allowed himself to cautiously criticize certain reforms (for example, the establishment of the office of fiscal), and he was suspected of secretly sympathizing with Tsarevich Alexei and the old Moscow regime.

In 1716, Peter I summoned his true companion, **the** encyclopedically educated **Feofan Prokopovich** (1681–1736), rector of the Kiev-Mohyla Academy and abbot of the Brotherhood Monastery in Podol (Fig. 3.2), to St. Petersburg. Prokopovich became not only the chief propagandist of Peter's reforms, but also an instrument of deepening church reform. In 1718, he was appointed bishop of Pskov, and in 1719–1720, he worked with the tsar on the compilation of **the Spiritual Regulations** (Fig. 3.3).

Fig. 3.2. Feofan Prokopovich

Fig. 3.3. Title page of Feofan Prokopovich's treatise "The Truth of the Monarch's Will" (1722)

---

[1] Valishevsky, K. Peter the Great. The Kingdom of Women. The Daughter of Peter the Great. Complete edition in one volume. Moscow, 2017. P. 381.

This document revealed the state of church life and justified the need for collegial governance. It "spoke of the ignorance of the clergy, the need to improve the living conditions of priests and monks, the decline of the Enlightenment, and the duty of bishops to eradicate all existing superstitions" (1).

In order to implement the necessary reforms, in 1721 **the Synod** was established as an administrative collegium consisting of 11 members: a president, two vice-presidents, four advisors, and four assessors. The representation of church hierarchs in it turned out to be very modest.

This purely bureaucratic body for the organization of the chancellery and paperwork resembled the senate and collegiums. In 1722, **a** special **chief prosecutor, Colonel I. V. Volgin**, was appointed to it, called upon to be "the eye of the sovereign" and "the steward of state affairs." As in the Senate, the prosecutor's office was staffed by spiritual fiscal inquisitors, who were called upon to secretly monitor the proper conduct of church life.

In accordance with the Spiritual Regulations, the Synod was called upon to monitor the accuracy of the text of spiritual books, eradicate superstitions, establish the authenticity of miracles performed by newly revealed icons and relics, observe the order of church services, combat schismatics and heretics, examine the merits of persons appointed as bishops, and protect the clergy from insults by secular lords."

The number of members of the Synod changed over time. For example, in 1763, at the beginning of Catherine's reign, it was limited to six members (three bishops, two archimandrites, and one protopope). In 1805, diocesan bishops began to be invited to attend meetings, taking turns and serving for terms ranging from one to three years. After 1819, the Metropolitans of Moscow and Kiev became permanent members by virtue of their positions. The metropolitan bishop was called the presiding member. The other members were called attendees.

In the absolutist state under Peter I and his successors, a decisive course was taken to deprive the church of its land ownership and serfs. By the middle of the 18th century, these were enormous riches. Only the serfs of the bishops' houses and monasteries of the Russian Empire numbered over 851 thousand

---

[1] Brikker, A. History of Peter the Great. History of Catherine II. Complete edition in one volume. Moscow, 2017. P. 444.

male souls in 20 thousand settlements (1). Due to bureaucratic delays and unforeseen circumstances, the nationalization process dragged on for several decades and was finally brought to an end **by Catherine II's decree of February 26, 1764**. According to this decree, the estates were transferred to the Board of Economy, and in return, the state allocated funds to finance church institutions in proportion to the amount of nationalized land. Many monasteries were closed or merged with others. A certain number of them were, as they say, "removed from the state," i.e., they were allowed to continue to exist, but without any state support. Thus, "after secularization, there remained in Great Russia 226 staffed and 161 non-staffed monasteries, for a total of 387 (not counting Siberia and Ukraine). At the same time, state subsidies to state-funded monasteries amounted to 207,750 rubles and 40 kopecks, whereas before the reform, the Church received 1,366,229 rubles from peasant rent alone from selected estates, not counting other estate **income**." (2).

The Church adapted to the new bureaucratic conditions of operation. During the 19th and early 20th centuries, the number of monasteries grew from 476 (1825) to 1,025 (1914), and their population increased from 11,000 to 94,600. "...The number of Orthodox monasteries grew particularly rapidly in the southern and eastern dioceses (Penza, Samara, Ufa, etc.). In the 19th century, the first monasteries appeared in the Orenburg diocese, Turkestan, and the Far **East**." (3)

In the 18th and 19th centuries, **St. Petersburg**, the young capital of the empire, became the center of Orthodoxy. In 1710, Peter I decided to build a monastery, and in 1713, the construction of its first church was completed. Thus**, the Holy Trinity Alexander Nevsky Lavra** was founded in the Holy Trinity Cathedral, where the relics of Alexander Nevsky rest (Fig. 3.4).

"The cathedral's sacred relics and venerated icons also include the icon of the Mother of God "Nevskaya Skoroplushnitsa", the icons of the Tikhvin,

---

[1] Lisovoy, N. N. The Eighteenth Century in the History of Russian Monasticism // Monasticism and Monasteries in Russia... p. 204.

[2] Ibid. pp. 209, 211, 212.

[3] Zyryanov P. N. Russian Monasteries and Monasticism in the 19th and Early 20th Centuries // Monasticism and Monasteries in Russia... P. 321, 322.

Fig. 3.4. Holy Trinity Alexander Nevsky Lavra

Fig. 3.5. Icon of the Mother of God "Nevskaya Skoroposlushnitsa"

Kazan and Iveron Mother of God, the venerated icon of the Holy Great Martyr Paraskeva Pyatnitsa, the icon of Alexander Nevsky with a particle of his relics" (1) (Figs. 3.5, 3.6).

In the 18th century, the following **cathedrals** were built in the northern capital: **the Nikolo-Bogo-Yavlenksy Maritime Cathedral** (Fig. 3.7) (which houses a particularly revered icon of St. Nicholas the Wonderworker, with part of his relics), **the Cathedral of the Vladimir Icon of the Mother of God** with a miraculous copy of the famous image (Figs. 3.8, 3.9), **the Cathedral of St. Andrew the First-Called Apostle with** a venerated icon of this saint (Fig. 3.10), **The TransFiguration Cathedral of the entire Guard** (Fig. 3.11), which houses the miraculous icon of the Mother of God "Joy of All Who Sorrow."

In the 19th century, St. Petersburg was adorned with **the Kazan Cathedral** (consecrated in 1811) and **the Cathedral of St. Isaac of Dalmatia** (opened in 1858) (Figs. 3.12, 3.13).

---

[1] Smirnov, P. T. Orthodox Shrines and Temples of St. Petersburg. St. Petersburg: Petrogradsky Publishing House, 2018. p. 5.

Icon of the Mother of God "Kazan"

Icon of the Mother of God of Tikhvin

Icon of St. Alexander Nevsky

Icon of the Holy Martyr Paraskeva Pyatnitsa

Fig. 3.6. Venerated icons of the Holy Trinity Alexander Nevsky Lavra[1]

---

[1] Venerated icons of the Holy Trinity Alexander Nevsky Lavra. URL: https://lavra.spb.ru/about/saints-and-shrines/2010-03-31-06-38-16/7-2010-03-31-08-05- 18.html

Fig. 3.7. St. Nicholas and Epiphany Naval Cathedral

Fig. 3.8. Cathedral of the Vladimir Icon of the Mother of God

Fig. 3.9. Vladimir Icon of the Mother of God

Fig. 3.10. Cathedral of St. Andrew the First-Called

Fig. 3.11. TransFiguration Cathedral of the entire Guard

Fig. 3.12. Kazan Cathedral

Fig. 3.13. Cathedral of St. Isaac of Dalmatia

***

Of course, the costs of Peter's Westernization and the subsequent inertial state policy towards the church could not destroy the high moral authority of Russian Orthodoxy. In the 17th and early 20th centuries, we encounter many examples of religious asceticism. In **the Sarov monastery,** and then for 15 years in the forest, the son of a Kursk merchant, St. **Seraphim** (1754–1833), prayed tirelessly. Upon returning to the monastery at the behest of heavenly forces, he came out of seclusion in 1825 and began to heal the mental and physical illnesses of those who turned to him (Fig. 3.14).

In St. Petersburg, after the death of her husband, a court singer, his 26-year-old widow **Ksenia** gave away all her possessions and became a city wanderer. Soon, those around her noticed that there was a deep meaning in her words and actions. When she entered a house, it was considered a good omen. Mothers rejoiced when Ksenia crossed their children or simply stroked their heads, convinced that a single touch from the Blessed One would bring healing. Cab drivers asked her to give them a ride, even if only a short one

Fig. 3.14. Venerable Seraphim of Sarov   Fig. 3.15. Xenia of St. Petersburg

with them, on such a day, income was guaranteed. The merchants at the market tried to give her a kalach or some other food, and if Blessed Ksenia took it, the goods were quickly sold out. Through her great humility, her feat of spiritual and physical poverty, her love for her neighbors, and her prayers Ksenia acquired the graceful gift of clairvoyance (Fig. 3.15).

Blessed Xenia died in the early 19th century and was buried in the Smolensk Cemetery in St. Petersburg, where during her lifetime she helped build a church in honor of the Smolensk Icon of the Mother of God. Her grave immediately became a place of worship, and in 1902 a new chapel was built over it, which is still a place of worship today.

In the 18th and 19th centuries, some old and new monasteries flourished. For example, **the TransFiguration Monastery on Valaam Island**, whose documented history begins in the 14th century, experienced its highest rise in the 19th century under the abbot Father Damaskin. Under his successor, Jonah II, the great cathedral, designed to accommodate more than 3 000 people.

---

[1] Akathist and Life of Saint Blessed Xenia of St. Petersburg. St. Petersburg, [no date]. pp. 30–31.

Fig. 3.16. The TransFiguration Monastery of Valaam

The Valaam ascetics wanted to turn their monastery into a New Jerusalem. By the beginning of World War I, about 1 000 people lived on the island (Fig. 3.16).

The Christmas-Virgin Mary Sanaksarsky Monastery was founded in 1659, three versts from the district town of Temnikov on the left bank of the Moksha River, but it was most famous in the 18th and early 21st centuries. The renowned Russian naval commander Admiral **Fyodor Ushakov,** who was canonized as a saint, spent several of his last years here in the village of Alekseevka, near the monastery (Fig. 3.17).

In essence, every provincial town is a center of religious life. Thus, in Penza, where during the reign of Nicholas I (1837) there were about 20 000 people (including 431 clergy, 953 civil servants, 6,307 townspeople, 1 985 lower military ranks, 6 229 state and 1,874 serf peasants, 45 teachers, and two midwives) (1). ·**the Spassky Cathedral** was built in 1824 (Fig. 3.18).

---

[1] Penza Provincial Gazette. January 20, 1839.

Fig. 3.17. The Nativity and Assumption Sanaksarsky Monastery

Fig. **3.18.** Spassky Cathedral in Penza at the beginning of the 20th century

It was visited by many members of the imperial family (including Alexander I and Nicholas I), and its main shrine was the miraculous Kazan Icon of the Mother of God, presented by Tsar Alexei Mikhailovich, which saved the city from a nomadic raid in 1717.

The cathedral is also associated with the end of the short but brilliant life of Bishop Innokenty (I. D. Smirnov) of Penza and Saratov (1784–1819) (Fig. 3.19).

Bishop Innokenty, who had previously taught at the St. Petersburg Theological Seminary and the St. Petersburg Theological Academy, was a leading expert on church history, and episcopal pe held the Skopskaya chair for just over two months. In 2000, he was canonized by the Russian Orthodox Church, and his relics are kept in the rebuilt Spassky Cathedral... (Figs. 3.20, 3.21).

Fig. 3.19. Bishop Innokenty (Smirnov)

***

Russia did not experience a Renaissance, but many researchers agree with the term "pre-Renaissance" proposed by D. S. Likhachev. Its specificity lies in the fact that humanistic ideals, interest in the inner spiritual world of man, the flourishing of art, and the growth of interest in rational knowledge were not accompanied in Russia by a process of secularization of culture." (1) However secularization came later, primarily under the influence **of Peter's Westernization.** "Even in church art, religious painting of the European type is spreading. Old Russian traditions are preserved only in part in the Old Believer milieu and in folk art" (2).

---

[1]Senyutkina, O. N., Shimanskaya, O. K., Parshakov, A. S., Samoilova, M. P. Culture. Religion. Tolerance. Cultural Studies: Textbook. 2nd ed. / Edited by O. N. Senyutkina. Moscow, 2022. P. 40.

[2] Ibid. p. 44.

Fig. 3.20. Contemporary view of the restored Spassky Cathedral

Fig. 3.21. Meeting between Patriarch Kirill
and Governor of the Penza Region O. V. Melnichenko

According to numerous historical observations, "the phases of the secularization cycle are as follows: total religiosity-de-ism — religious indifference (atheism) — religious syncretism (mysticism) — pantheism — revived church religiosity or secularization." At the same time, in Russia, the process of Europeanization merged with the process of secularization, and "following the nobility, new strata of educated society, the nascent **Russian intelligentsia**, became involved in this process." (1)

Apparently, the decisive moment in the secularization of the nobility was the Age of Enlightenment.

Peter I also laid the foundations for dominant guardianship, state legislation, church reform, and education. "During the first half of the 18th century, various elements of Western culture (everyday, technical, political, philosophical, etc.) were introduced into Russia. Against this backdrop, in the second half of the 18th century, the phenomenon of Russian noble culture emerged, and as a result, Russia's own philosophical and educational schools of thought appeared." (2). At the same time· the flourishing of secular culture in the second half of the 18th century did not mean a shift toward religious indifference. "All secular educational institutions had Orthodox churches. By the end of the 18th century, God's law had taken an important place in education, and spiritual censorship was in effect." (3)

Elements of secularism were brought into the public consciousness by active publishing and young journalism. The circulation of the first private magazines (Trudolyubivaya Pchela [The Hardworking Bee], Zhivopisets [The Painter], "Truten," "Friend of Honest People," "Spirit Mail," "Spectator," etc.) were small and short-lived (4), but their target audience (the educated aristocratic elite) was also very limited in number.

---

[1] Sinelina, Yu. Yu. Secularization in the Social History of Russia // Monitoring Public Opinion. 2004.№ 1. pp. 85, 86.

[2] Ivakhnenko E. N. Education, Science, and Religion in the Russian Enlightenment in Search of Compromise (Part 1) // Bulletin of the Russian State University for the Humanities. Series: Philosophy. Sociology. Art Studies. 2017. pp. 288, 289.

[3] Starodubtsev M. P. Current values of the ideal of man in the understanding of the Russian nobility of the 18th century: transformation of judgments // News of the Russian State Pedagogical University named after A. I. Herzen. 2012. № 152. P. 210.

[4] Tugova L. N., Bijieva Z. S. M., Ordokova A. Yu. The Age of Russian Enlightenment and the Formation of Russian Journalism // World of Science, Culture, Education. 2020. No. 4. Pp. 362–364.

Fig. 3.22. Catherine II and the cultural elites of Russia

In one way or another, "the Age of Enlightenment initiated the creation of a new type of intelligentsia, well-educated, following events in Europe and striving to create a new national ideology imbued with secular, worldly principles." (1) Empress **Catherine II** herself and her entourage (**I. I. Betskoy, E. R. Dashkova**), publishers **N. I. Novikov, A. P. Sumarokov,** historian, prince, and major general **M. M. Shcherbatov,** playwright **D. I. Fonvizin, and** Metropolitan of Moscow and Kolomna **Platon (Levshin)** promoted the cult of knowledge (Fig. 3.22).

***

The proclamation of Russia as an empire in 1721 and its subsequent successes in expansion — primarily in the western and southern directions — could not fail to instill **a sense of imperial scale** in the public consciousness.

But this feeling had nothing to do with **aggressive hegemony** or a desire to rise above other states. Nor did it have any of the characteristics of **providential exceptionalism** or divine election that are typical of Americans, for example. Several segments can be distinguished in the Russian colonization flow: "free colonization," in which fugitive serfs, deserting soldiers, and persecuted sectarians participated; "military **colonization**"; "monastic **colonization**";... "Cossack colonization..." (2). However, in all cases, there was no question of severing ties with the Fatherland, as was the case with Western European settlers. (3)

In Russia, "the absorption of the Asian periphery can be represented not only as a gradual expansion of the Russian national core, but also as the creation of Russian enclaves, islands of the 'Russian world' in strategic areas of Russian Asia. From the second half of the 19th century, the movement of the Russian population to the imperial peripheries (both spontaneous and regulated by the state) began to be perceived by the government and society as

---

[1] Grinenko, G. V., Sinyavina, N. V. Russian Enlightenment as a cultural function of the domestic intelligentsia in the 1750s–1800s // Bulletin of Moscow State University of Culture and Arts. 2017.№ 6. P. 32.

[2] Etkind A. Internal Colonization. Russia's Imperial Experience. Moscow: New Literary Review, 2013. P. 101.

[3] Kaufman, A. A. Resettlement and Colonization: State Policy and Peasant Land Ownership in Post-Reform Russia. Moscow: Librokom, 2012. p. 5.

purposeful political and national construction of the empire. This was a kind of super-task, which from the 1860s onwards was formulated as a new strategic course for the creation of a "united and indivisible" Russia. (1)

***

Undoubtedly, a sense **of imperial security** gradually took shape in the mass consciousness, facilitated both by successes in the wars of the 18th and 19th centuries and by faith in the state icons that were the guardians of the Russian Land. According to believers: "**The Tikhvin Icon** protects and blesses the northern borders. **The Iver Icon** protects the southern borders. **The Pochaev Icon and the Smolensk** Icon protect the Russian land from the west. In the east, **the Kazan Icon of the Mother of God** shines with rays of grace, protecting the Russian lands to the ends of the earth. And in the center shines **the image of the Vladimir Mother of God.**" (2).

The Vladimir Icon of the Mother of God is the oldest. Its author is considered to be the evangelist Luke, and a copy of the icon came to Russia in the 12th century, sent by the Patriarch of Constantinople to the Grand

Fig. 3.23. Vladimir Icon of the Mother of God

Prince of Kiev. From 1160, the miraculous image was kept in Vladimir, and in 1395 it was transferred to Moscow. It is believed that it not only repeatedly saved our homeland from invaders, but also healed heart and eye diseases, contributed to happy marriages, and freed people from sinful thoughts and turmoil (Fig. 3.23).

The Tikhvin Icon of the Mother of God, which appeared from Byzantium in 1383, is associated in the eyes of believers with Russia's special mission as the Third Rome. In particular, the founders of the Russian Land in the 16th century, Vasily II and Ivan the Terrible, turned to her.

Since 2004, after long wanderings,

---

[1] Remnev, A. V., Suvorova, N. G. Colonization of Asian Russia: Imperial and National Scenarios of the Second Half of the 19th Century and Early 20th Century. Omsk: Nauka, 2013. P. 16.

[2] "Icons Guarding the Russian Land" — Three Icons That Saved Russia. URL: https://moiarussia.ru/ikony-na-strazhe-zemli-russkoj/ (accessed on March 31, 2022).

Fig. 3.24. Tikhvin Icon of the Mother of God

Fig. 3.25. Smolensk Icon of the Mother of God (Dionysius, 1482)

begun during the Great Patriotic War, it returned to its permanent location — the Tikhvin Monastery of the Dormition of the Mother of God (Fig. 3.24).

A miraculous copy of **the** famous **Iveron Icon of the Mother of God**, located on Mount Athos since the 11th century, appeared much later in Russia, in 1648. At that time, the protection of the southern borders was of utmost strategic importance for Russia.

The Pochaev Icon of the Mother of God, unlike other images venerated in Russian Orthodoxy, is also worshipped by believers of other Slavic peoples. In a sense, it is a symbol of the integrity of the Slavic world. According to legend, it was given to the monks of the Holy Dormition Pavlovsk Lavra (now located in the Ternopil region of Ukraine) by a noblewoman who received it as a gift in 1559 from the future Patriarch of Constantinople, who was passing by. Many miracles are associated with the icon, in particular, the deliverance of the monastery from the Turkish siege in 1675, as well as the healing of those who turned to it from incurable diseases (up to 600 cases have been recorded).

Unfortunately, the location of **the Smolensk Icon of the Mother of God,** which guarded Russia's western borders in the 12th century, has been unknown since 1943 (Fig. 3.25). Prior to that, under Vladimir Monomakh, it was transferred to the Smolensk Cathedral Church in honor of the Assumption

Fig. 3.26. Kazan Icon of the Most Holy Mother of God

In the first half of the 19th century, the icon briefly found its way to Moscow, w h e r e two copies were made, one of which ended up in the Blagoveshchensk Cathedral of the Kremlin, and the other in the Novodevichy Convent. Another copy was reproduced in 1602.

The icon of the Kazan Mother of God, found in Kazan in 1579, is considered the most revered in Russia. And this is no coincidence. It was this icon that accompanied the People's Militia of K. Minin and D. Pozharsky during the liberation of Moscow (Fig. 3.26).

Hundreds of churches and monasteries are now dedicated to the Kazan icon monasteries scattered throughout Russian cities. In particular, one of the copies of the icon has been in the Kazan Cathedral in St. Petersburg since 1811. The Moscow copy is located in the Kazan Cathedral on Nikolskaya Street. As for the original, its fate was already unclear in the 19th century. There are versions that it was stolen in 1904 from the Kazan Monastery of the Mother of God.

***

For the multinational Russian Empire, "until the beginning of the 20th century, there was a closer fusion of religion and law than in other countries" (1). This state religious paternalism was entirely justified, since Orthodox Christianity was used by the authorities to stabilize domestic political relations in the context of the existence of fairly large enclaves of foreign populations. According to the 1897 census, there were just over 87 million Orthodox Christians, or 69.3 % of the population, Catholics and Lutherans accounted for 9.15% and 2.83% respectively, and Jews accounted for 4.2%. The largest foreign community, accounting for 11.1%, was Muslim (2).

---

[1] Kuliev, F. M. Legal regulation of religious activities in the Russian Empire in the late 18th and early 20th centuries // Izvestiya SOIGSI. 2015.№ 15. P. 18.

[2] Rubakin, N. A. Russia in Figures. Country. People. Estates. Classes (based on official and scientific research). St. Petersburg, 1912.

In legal terms, Orthodox Christianity enjoyed a privileged position. "Only Orthodox Christians were given the right to propagate their teachings..." They had no restrictions on the public nature of religious ceremonies. "Conversion to Orthodoxy was accompanied by all kinds of incentives and, above all, exemption from paying all or some taxes. At the same time, the state controlled the practical aspects of the life of Orthodox church organizations. It determined the governing bodies of various denominations, the duties and punishments of the clergy" (1).

Based on political and ideological considerations, each of the beliefs alternative to Orthodoxy was assigned its own place in the bureaucratic management system. "The upper echelons of the religious structure of the population of the Russian Empire, after the Orthodox, were occupied by Christian religions — Roman Catholic (from the Hernhuters to the Reformers and Lutherans), Armenian Gregorian, and Armenian Catholic. They were followed in terms of privileges by Talmudists, Shiite and Sunni Muslims, and Karaite Jews. Next came the spiritual administrations of the Kalmyk and Buryat peoples" (2).

Schismatics and sectarians were recognized as a public danger and socially undesirable. In Articles 196, 197, and 203 of the "Code of Criminal and Corrective Punishments," they were classified as

1) less harmful in civil terms;

2) particularly harmful both in terms of faith and in civil terms;

3) combined with fierce fanaticism and fanatical encroachment on their own lives and those of others (3).

The authorities had no other statistics on schismatics and sectarians, since the latter did not publicize their activities, and parish priests underestimated the number of religious dissidents for the sake of their own careers. It is known however, for example, in the mid-1820s, the Ministry of

---

[1] Dorskaya, A. A. The legal status of subjects of the Russian Empire in the early 20th century: the religious aspect // News of the Russian State Pedagogical University named after A. I. Herzen. 2002.№ 4. pp. 214, 215.

[2] Safonov, A. A. Regulation of the activities of non-Orthodox and non-Christian religions by the Ministry of Internal Affairs // Bulletin of the Perm State University named after N. A. Nekrasov. 2006.№ 5. P. 32.

[3] Baturkin, A. Religious Policy of the Russian Empire in the Second Half of the 19th Century // Vlast. 2009.№ 2. pp. 4–5.

Internal Affairs estimated the number of schismatics at 1 million, and in 1862, at 8 million (1).

Not without reason, the well-known public Figure I. S. Aksakov asked: "Where does such spiritual malleability of the Russian Orthodox person come from? ... Is it not because this Russian person is deprived of any religious education whatsoever? That his attitude towards Orthodoxy is often mundane...". (2) In any case, the presence of a significant number of subjects who deviated from official Orthodoxy testified to a certain spiritual malaise in the empire, which the authorities in the 1830s attempted to resolve not only through administrative measures, but also through ideological and organizational measures.

Fig. 3.27. S. S. Uvarov

The official theory of populism, concentrated in the formula **Orthodoxy-Autocracy-Nationality**, was articulated at the most opportune moment when Europe was becoming engrossed in liberal revolutions and the appointment of S. S. Uvarov as Minister of Education in 1833. into the post of Minister of Education, was voiced at an extremely opportune moment — at a time when Europe was becoming enthralled with liberal revolutions and threatening to destabilize the social order in the Russian Empire (Fig. 3.27). Two years before S. S. Uvarov's appointment, Emperor Nicholas I, based on the realities of the Polish uprising of 1830–1831, introduced restrictions on educational contacts with Europe. In particular, young people were not allowed to study abroad under the age of 18, so as not to be exposed to the harmful influences of the European Enlightenment.

But at the same time, Uvarov's formula, for all its outward patriotism, was the product of soulless monarchical bureaucracy. It continued the tradition of the 18th century with its utilitarian legitimization of autocracy as an instrument, creating and preserved the state.

---

[1] Olenin, T. S. The Problem of Classifying Russian Religious Sectarianism in the Russian Empire // Izvestiya VUZov. North Caucasus Region. Social Sciences. Appendix. 2005.№ 2. pp. 15–16.

[2] Aksakov I. S. On the Truth of Russian Politics // Complete Works. Moscow, 1886. pp. 356–357.

There was no question of any sacred monarchical nature. He interpreted Orthodoxy from the standpoint of a guarantee of social and family happiness.

Uvarov defined the Russian nation not as a people, but as a community with a characteristic of boundless devotion to its rulers, which distinguished Russians from Europeans, who were corrupted by the philosophy of the Enlightenment (1).

Nicholas I himself, while demonstrating his love for Russian history and monuments of Russian antiquity, encouraging national style in church architecture and music, and attaching special significance to his trips to Moscow as evidence of the people's love for the emperor, was at the same time not ready for the symbols "peasant nationality" or the everyday rapprochement between the peasantry and the nobility. It is characteristic that when some public Figures (Khomakov, Aksakov, and others) grew beards, the Ministry of Internal Affairs issued a reprimand, since for the emperor this detail of appearance was associated with radicalism and Judaism.

Nevertheless, **even the authorities' not entirely full-fledged attempt to "distance themselves" from the West coincided with the desire of many representatives of the nobility in the second half of the 1830s to resist the admiration of Europe.**

It should be noted that this patriotic movement had a small but influential group of conservative predecessors at the beginning of the 19th century. On the eve of the Patriotic War of 1812 and during the war itself, it counteracted the fashionable Gallomania among the Russian nobility and focused attention on the disastrous consequences of the French Revolution of the late 18th century, achieving key positions in power for a short time. The soul of the circle of conservative realists was the emperor's sister, **Grand Duchess Ekaterina Pavlovna.** State Secretary **A. S. Shishkov,** who took the second highest position in the state after the resignation of the liberal M. M. Speransky, became the author of most of the tsar's manifestos addressed to the people. Governor-General of Moscow **F. V. Rostopchin**, the organizer of the Moscow fire and author of patriotic, anti-French posters, played a role in Napoleon's flight from ravaged Moscow. The publisher of Russky Vestnik, **S. N. Glinka,** established himself as a Fighter against French cultural expansion in Russian society. The Minister of War and outstanding artilleryman, organizer of military settlements hated by the peasants, **A. A. Arakcheev** was

---

[1] Zorin, A. L. The Ideology of "Orthodoxy, Autocracy, and Nationality": An Attempt at Reconstruction // New Literary Review. 1996.№ 26. pp. 92–101.

Grand Duchess
Ekaterina Pavlovna

A. S. Shishkov

S. N. Glinka

A. A. Arakcheev

N. M. Karamzin

Fig. 3.28. Russian conservatives of the first quarter of the 19th century.

highly valued by Emperors Paul I and Alexander I and played a significant role in strengthening the country's defense capabilities. Historian **N. M. Karamzin**, author of the 12-volume History of the Russian State, justified the idea of absolute monarchy and criticized the slightest deviations from this line (Fig. 3.28).

***

The Slavophiles are trying to restore the foundations of national spiritual culture. **Alexei Stepanovich Khomyakov** (1804–1860), a descendant of an ancient noble family, is considered the founder of this directions (Fig. 3.29).

His service in the army did not prevent him from becoming interested in poetry, painting, journalism, and theology. In 1839, in his article "On the Old and the New," he put forward the main tenets of Slavophilism. Discussing the negative and positive experiences of Russia's development, the author asserts its originality and advantages over the West. "Our early history is not stained by conquest. Blood and enmity did not serve as the foundation of the Russian state... The Church, limiting the scope of its activities, never lost the purity of its inner life and did not teach its children lessons of injustice and violence." At present, the publicist continues, "we will move forward boldly and unerringly, taking up the accidental discoveries of the West, but giving them a deeper meaning or revealing in them those human principles that have remained hidden from the West..." (1)

A. S. Khomyakov laid the foundation for a religious-philosophical understanding of conciliarity in Russian social thought. He understood this phenomenon, as his eldest son D. A. Khomakov, as a kind of common feeling among believers, as "the free unity of the Church in their joint understanding of the truth and their joint search for the path to salvation, a unity based on unanimous love for Christ and divine righteousness." (2)

"In Orthodox Christianity, A. S. Khomyakov was the first secular religious thinker. He paved the way for free religious philosophy, liberated from scholasticism. He showed by his own example that the gift of teaching, in its conciliarity, belongs to every member of the church, and not only to the spiritual hierarchy." (3)

Ivan Vasilyevich Kireevsky (1806–1807), a native of the Tula province (Fig. 3.30), was practically the same age as Khomyakov. He began his service in the Moscow Archives of the Collegium of Foreign Affairs in 1823 and lived abroad for a short time, where he attended lectures by Hegel and Schelling. His experience of publishing the magazine The European in 1832 ended with the banning of the article "The Nineteenth Century," in which the authorities saw a demand for a constitution for Russia.

---

[1] URL: dugward.ru/library/nikolay1/homjakov_star_nov.html (accessed: 15.01.2021).

[2] Mishchenko, A. V. On Sobornost as a Spiritual, Religious, and Philosophical Concept // Vestnik MGTU. 2011. Vol. 14, p№ 2. p. 321.

[3] Lipich T. I., Rubezhansky S. I. Orthodox patriotism of A. S. Khomyakov: philosophical, cultural and theological contexts // NOMOTHETIKA: Philosophy. Sociology. Law. 2015.№ 3.

Fig. 3.29. Alexei Stepanovich Khomyakov

Fig. 3.30. Ivan Vasilyevich Kireevsky

Under the influence of his wife, Kireevsky embarked on the path of ecclesiastical life. His mentors were **Filaret**, an elder of the Novospassky Monastery in Moscow, and **Makarii**, an elder of the Optina Hermitage. Ivan Vasilyevich found his calling in translating the works of the Holy Fathers of the Church into modern Russian and publishing them.

In his articles "In Response to A. S. Khomyakov" (1839), "On the Nature of Education in Europe and Its Relationship to Education in Russia" (1852), "On the Necessity of New Principles for Philosophy" (1856), he criticized the Western rationalist tradition and contrasted it with the integrity of spirit and conciliar personality in Russia (1).

Kireevsky believed that rationalism and individualism had not taken root in our country. "On the contrary, under the influence of the Orthodox Church, communal organization of society and collectivist morality prevailed here. The Church played an important educational role in Russia: it formed and spread moral values that became customary for the entire Russian people..."

According to Kireevsky, Russian statehood was formed peacefully — through the voluntary invitation of the Varangians.

"Thanks to this, Russian society developed gradually, evolutionarily, without a rigid class structure or acute political struggle...

---

[1] Dronov, I. E. Kireevsky, Ivan Vasilyevich. URL: https:// w.histrf.ru/articles/article/show/kirieievskii_ivan_vasilievich (accessed: 25.01.2021).

The center of ancient Kireevsky considered the center of non-Russian society to be not a castle, but a monastery, not the embodiment of power, but a symbol of morality. The split of the church into factions in the 16th century brought the state to a leading role and paved the way for the reign of Peter I, during which "the country went from the extreme of self-isolation to the extreme of imitation." (1).

The Aksakov brothers, who belonged to the same circle of Moscow nobility, played a prominent role in the development of Slavophilism. **Konstantin Sergeyevich Aksakov** (1817–1864) is even considered the leader and ideologist of this social movement (Fig. 3.31). A graduate of Moscow University in 1835, he became close to A. S. Khomyakov and I. V. Kireevsky and began to collaborate with such publications as Telescope, Rumor, Moscow Observer, and Domestic Notes. In the early 1840s, he entered into a polemic with literary critic V. G. Belinsky and reviewed individual volumes of S. M. Solovyov's history of Russia. In 1848, he wrote a letter to Emperor Nicholas I calling for an end to Westernization, and in 1856, he addressed Alexander II with a "Memorandum on the Internal State of Russia," in which he condemned bribery and serfdom and advocated for the convening of a Zemsky Sobor. He also formulated several characteristics of belonging to the Slavophile doctrine: "the foundation of our entire spiritual, intellectual, and moral existence is preserved in our Orthodox Church; sympathy for the Russian people; love for Moscow; sympathy for the 'Slavic tribes'" (2).

His younger brother, **Ivan Sergeevich Aksakov** (1823–1886), graduated from law school in St. Petersburg and ended up working in the Senate, where he took an active part in various senate investigations. Upon his retirement in 1851, he became actively involved in the publishing activities of the Slavophiles. After moving abroad, he met A. I. Herzen and became his secret correspondent. In 1861–1862, he edited the newspaper Den, and in 1867–1868, he published the newspaper Moskva. Like many of his comrades in the movement, he suffered from censorship restrictions (Fig. 3.32).

After the death of his elder brother Ivan Sergeevich together with Yu. F. Samarin in the 1860s–1870s became the leader of the Slavophilism.

---

[1] Shpagin, S. A. Russia and the West in the Philosophy of I. V. Kireevsky (on the 200th anniversary of his birth) // Bulletin of Tomsk State University. 2007. № 296. P. 79.

[2] Myrikova, A. V., Shirinyants, A. A. The Social and Political Views of K. S. Aksakov (bibliographic essay). Article One // Bulletin of Moscow University. Ser. 12. Political Sciences. 2010.№ 2. P. 42.

Fig. 3.31. Konstantin Sergeyevich Aksakov

Fig. 3.32. Ivan Sergeyevich Aksakov

"By publishing Slavophile newspapers in the 1860s, Aksakov made a name for himself in journalistic circles. And rightly so: he had a journalistic temperament and a sharp pen... He promoted Slavophile views more energetically than his ideologues." (1)

Yuri Fedorovich Samarin (1819–1876), who came from a noble and wealthy family of a colonel, also began his career in the Senate (Fig. 3.33). After retiring in 1853 and taking over the management of his estates, he came to the conclusion that serfdom should be abolished, and submitted a memorandum on this subject, an abridged version of which was published in the journal Selskoe Blagoustroystvo (Rural Improvement). During the preparation of the peasant reform, Samarin was a member of the Samara Provincial Committee, and in the early 1860s, as part of a government commission, he studied the peasant question in the Kingdom of Poland. Advocating for Russia's independent development, he also defended reasonable innovations borrowed from abroad. He was a supporter of the Zemsky Sobor, judicial reform, and freedom of the press, but at the same time continued the traditions of the older generation of Slavophiles and was a supporter of the people's monarchies.

---

[1] Motin S. V. Ivan Sergeevich Aksakov — jurist, publicist, Slavophile, and public Figure // Gaps in Russian legislation. Legal Journal. 2016. No. 4.

Fig. 3.33. Yuri Fedorovich Samarin

Fig. 3.34. Alexander Ivanovich Koshelev

Fig. 3.35. Fyodor Vasilyevich Chizhov

The Slavophiles A. I. Koshelev and F. S. Chizhov (Figs. 3.34, 3.35) turned out to be people of a special, entrepreneurial disposition. **Alexander Ivanovich Koshelev** (1806–1883), nephew of the Tambov governor and son of an adjutant general, after serving in Moscow and St. Petersburg, was involved in wine procurement until 1848, and then wholesale trade in bread, supplying it to the army and navy. On his estates (5 500 serfs), he ran a diversified farm, established a secular administration, built several schools, and purchased agricultural machinery. He repeatedly appealed to the government with initiatives, including on the peasant question, which were reasonable and consistent in nature (for example, the redemption of peasants with all their land within 12 years). Koshelev's funds were used to publish the Slavophile magazine Beseda, the works of I. V. Kireevsky, and the weekly Zemstvo, which defended the values of the peasant community and criticized the financial and economic activities of the government in 1880–1882.

Fyodor Vasilyevich Chizhov (1811–1817), an organizer of railway construction and philanthropist, achieved no less success in the field of entrepreneurship. Unlike other Slavophiles, he could not boast of a brilliant noble pedigree. After graduating from St. Petersburg University, he managed to obtain a master's degree in mathematics, but by 1840 his interests had already shifted to the humanities. Upon returning to St. Petersburg in 1846 after a long stay abroad, Chizhov noted that, apart from the tsar, his family, and the people, everyone in the city was cosmopolitan (1).

In Moscow, he became acquainted with a circle of Slavophiles, whom he criticized for their inertia and primitive resistance to everything European. According to Chizhov, the technological and educational experience of the West should be adopted. In particular, he was a great enthusiast of higher engineering and professional technical education.

After being sent into exile in Ukraine, Chizhov got the chance to take on a serious business project. He leased 60 acres of silk plantations. Later, he entered the railway business, becoming a co-founder of the Moscow-Troitsk Railway Company, which intended to build a 66-verst railway line to Sergiev Posad. The route was later extended to Yaroslavl and Vologda. Moscow capitalists elected Chizhov as chairman of the board of the Moscow-Kursk Railway. In 1866, he also headed the Moscow Merchant Bank, and from 1806 to 1869, the Moscow Merchant Society for Mutual Credit. On Chizhov's initiative and with his participation, the northern outskirts were developed a steamship company was organized for navigation on the White Sea and the Arctic Ocean.

---

[1] Simonova, I. Fedor Chizhov. Moscow: Molodaya Gvardiya, 2002. p. 15.

He was involved in entrepreneurial and social publishing activities. From 1858 to 1861, together with I. K. Babst, he published the newsletter "Industry," which included a supplement dedicated to industry and trade, "Akcioner," and in 1867, he founded the political and economic newspaper "Moscow." In matters of economic policy, he adhered to sound protectionist views. He criticized the attraction of adventurous foreign capital to Russia to the detriment of domestic entrepreneurs. Overall, the Slavophiles were few in number. Along with the founders (A. S. Khomyakov, I. V. Kireevsky, P. V. Kireevsky), in the 1840s, their friends and followers (A. I. Koshelev, N. M. Yazykov, D. A. Valiev, K. S. Aksakov, Yu. F. Samarin, A. N. Popov, V. A. Panov, F. V. Chizhov, I. S. Aksakov, V. A. Yeligin), whom the authorities treated with great suspicion and carried out a number of short-term detentions. Many of their works were banned by censorship. "There was no doubt in the minds of government officials about the opposition of the Slavophile circle, although the depth of this opposition was measured in different ways. In the 1860s, few dignitaries would have thought of the Slavophiles as "reds"...". At the same time, "a firm belief in the liberalism of the Slavophiles coexisted in government circles with a tolerant attitude towards them" (1).

***

The patriotic aspirations of the Slavophiles were opposed by the more confused and contradictory ideas **of the Westernizers**, who idealized the achievements of the West. Ideologically and culturally, this social movement was more diverse than Slavophilism. There were Westernizers-liberals and Westernizers-socialists. There were powerful sections of professors and writers. Incidentally, this social movement apparently outnumbered its opponents.

The strangest and most unacceptable point of view was published by **Pyotr Yakovlevich Chaadaev** (1794–1856) in 1836 — a fashionable dandy and Freemason who was declared insane by Emperor Nicholas I (Fig. 3.36). His phrase, "We live in the present, within its narrowest limits, without a past or future, amid dead stagnation," reveals the nature of the author's position.

---

[1] Tsimbaev, N. I. Slavophilism: From the History of Russian Social and Political Thought of the 19th Century. Moscow, 1986. pp. 122, 128–134.

Fig. 3.36. Pyotr Yakovlevich Chaadaev

Chaadaev gave a completely unfair assessment of Russia: "Standing between the two main parts of the world, the East and the West, leaning with one elbow on China and the other on Germany, we should have combined in ourselves both great principles of spiritual nature: imagination and reasoning, and combined in our civilization the history of the entire globe. But this is not the role assigned to us by fate Historical experience does not exist for us; generations and centuries have passed without benefit to us. Looking at us, one might say that the general law of humanity has been abolished in relation to us. Alone in the world, we have given nothing to the world, taught it nothing; we have not contributed a single idea to the mass of human ideas humanity, we have contributed nothing to the progress of the human mind, and we have distorted everything we have gained from this progress." (1).

Chaadaev extolled Catholicism and lamented the schism between it and Orthodoxy, which, he claimed, had deprived Russia of the fruits of social progress. However, in the 1840s, he softened his skepticism somewhat: he now viewed Russia's isolation from historical progress as an advantage that would allow it to reach the level of Western civilization while avoiding its inherent vices.

Westernism initially began to take shape around the Moscow circle of historian and professor **T. N. Granovsky** (1813–1855) (Fig. 3.37). Coming from a small noble family, he graduated from the law faculty of St. Petersburg University, but went on to teach history at Moscow University. His lectures, based on a dialectical approach to the past, were hugely successful, as was the young teacher himself, who did not neglect personal communication with his students. A circle of young university teachers and lawyers formed around him, including N. I. Krylov, P. G. Redkin, K. D. Kavelin (Fig. 3.38), philosopher and antiquarian D. L. Kryukov, and historian P. N. Kudryavtsev. Defending the universality of historical laws, the lecturer effectively declared that the

---

[1] Zorin, A. Westernizers, Slavophiles, and Others: Debates on Russia's Path. URL: https://arzamas.academy/materials/1384 (accessed: 24.01.2021).

Fig. 3.37. T. N. Granovsky   Fig. 3.38. K. D. Kavelin

ideas of parliamentarism and revolutionary uprisings were not European inventions, but objective processes (1). "The West has worked out its history with bloody sweat, and we are getting the fruits of it almost for free, so what right do we have not to love it?" asked T. N. Granovsky (2).

Over time, **the Westernizing movement grew stronger and more diverse**. The uncompromising, revolutionary positions were taken by former adherents of Westernism **V. G. Belinsky** (1811–1848), **A. I. Herzen** (1812–1870), **N. P. Ogarev** (1813–1877), who had lost their former enthusiasm for the West. Thus, V. G. Belinsky rightly wrote in one of his articles in 1847 that it was possible to take an interest in European issues, "but at the same time it would be completely futile for us to accept these issues as our own." In turn, A. I. Herzen noted with sarcasm in 1850 that in the West, "a beggar enjoys the same civil rights as Rothschild" (3).

---

[1] Beloved historian. Timofey Granovsky: a brilliant professor who did not engage in science // Kommersant. Money. 2016.№ 40. P. 43.

[2] Westernizers of the 1840s: N. V. Stankevich, V. G. Belinsky, A. I. Herzen, T. N. Granovsky, and others. Moscow, 1910. P. 215.

[3] Blecher, L. I., Lyubarsky, G. Yu. The Main Debate: From Westernizers and Slavophiles to Globalism and the New Middle Ages. Moscow, 2003. pp. 112, 113.

And yet the ranks of liberal Russian Westernizers continued to grow. After Granovsky's death, Moscow Westernizers V. P. Botkin, E. F. Korsch, S. M. Solovyov, and B. N. Chicherin united around the writer A. V. Stankevich (1821–1912). In St. Petersburg, under the leadership of young officials N. A. Milyutin and D. A. Milyutin, a second group of Westernizers was formed. Another Westernizing community formed around **K. D. Kavelin** (1818–1885), who had moved to St. Petersburg. Incidentally, Kavelin himself, a teacher of such a staunch Westernizer as B. N. Chicherin, became closer to the Slavophiles in the late 1850s and subsequently rejected both Westernism and Slavophilism.

He came to hold the view that "the views of Westernizers and Slavophiles are anachronisms. Now only one view is possible — a national, Russian view based on the study of real phenomena in the life of the Russian land..." (1). He interpreted this reality as the special role of the state in Russian history.

Indeed, serfdom and attitudes toward Peter I's reforms were long considered the main stumbling blocks in disputes between Westernizers and Slavophiles. By the early 1860s, the peasant question had been resolved — regardless of one's attitude toward the Great Peasant Reform of 1861. As for the disputes over the benefits of Peter's reforms, they lost their novelty and intensity over time. Russia was now living in a new, post-reform reality of unfolding modernization, and it was difficult to give a clear answer to the question of whether our country was with or without the West. After all, the situation was constantly changing.

Even prominent Russian historians had ambiguous attitudes toward Westernization (Fig. 3.39). S. M. Solovyov (1820–1879), professor (since 1848) and rector of Moscow University in 1871–1877, sympathized with Westernizers but agreed with Slavophiles on religion and faith, and on the historical calling of the Russian people. Along with the monumental 29-volume History of the Russian State, which was published between 1851 and 1879, he was also the author of the conservative-patriotic work History of the Fall of Poland (1863).

Another Russian historian, V. O. Klyuchevsky (1841–1911), who published A Course in History, was a student of S. M. Solovyov. At the same time, the scholar rejected the legal fetishism of B. N. Chicherin, which was

---

[1] Korsakov, D. A. K. D. Kavelin. Materials for a biography. From family correspondence and memoirs // Vestnik Evropy. 1886.№ 11. P. 189.

S. M. Solovyov   V. O. Klyuchevsky   S. F. Platonov

Fig. 3.39. Prominent Russian historians

fashionable at the time in the state school system and gave preference to political factors (1). He is also known for his criticism of the pro-Western enthusiasms of the Russian authorities in the 18th–19th centuries, who used the means of Western European culture against the freedom of the people (2).

The foremost researcher of the Time of Troubles, who taught history to members of the ruling family and was dean of the History and Philology Faculty at St. Petersburg University from 1900 to 1905. S. F. Platonov (1860–1933) was influenced by V. O. Klyuchevsky (3) and was a monarchist in his views. In his interpretation of Russian history, he proceeded from the "military character" of the Muscovite state, which fought on three fronts and was forced to enslave the estates. The final step in the emancipation of the estates was the Peasant Reform of 1861, which, however, did not lead to the acquisition of political rights, but stimulated excesses of radicalism. At the same time, the historian did not resemble his pro-Western colleagues and did not demand blind copying of European experience.

Meanwhile, **at the turn of the 1850s and 1860s, Westernizers came to power for the first time as an organized and united group**. This was no longer a cultural, everyday, and philosophical passion, but rather attempt to

---

[1] Asonov, N. V. Klyuchevsky as a historian and political scientist // Humanities. Bulletin of the Financial University. 2021.№ 11. P. 147.

[2] Klyuchevsky V. O. Works: in 9 vols. Moscow, 1990. P. 360.

[3] Mamontova, M. A. The Model of Historical Research in the View of S. F. Platonov // Bulletin of Omsk University. 2001.№ 1. P. 46.

Fig. 3.40. Grand Duke Konstantin Nikolaevich

Fig. 3.41. N. A. Milyutin

implement a targeted state policy. This was facilitated by Russia's defeat in the Crimean War and the accession of the new emperor Alexander II to the throne, the expectation of reforms on the part of a significant part of society, and the weakening of censorship restrictions in 1856–1861.

A circle of reformist administrators gathered around the tsar's younger brother, the decisive and impulsive Grand Duke **Konstantin Nikolayevich** (Fig. 3.40), a general admiral and minister of the navy who revived the Russian navy and patronized the arts and literature (1). This circle included government officials who were perceived differently by public opinion: for example, the "red" Deputy Minister of Internal Affairs **N. A. Milyutin** (Fig. 3.41) and the aristocrat Minister of the same department **P. A. Valuev** (Fig. 3.42). The Mikhailovsky Palace **of Grand Duchess Elena Pavlovna** (Fig. 3.43), patroness of N. A. Milyutin and the entire peasant emancipation movement, served as a secular "platform" for the development of reforms.

There is no doubt that the reformers of The era of Alexander II (especially before the start of the Polish uprising of 1863–1864) played an important role in the positive transformations of Russia. But this same era, which marked a cultural and ideological rapprochement with the West, also revealed **the dark side of capitalist progress,** manifested in the growth of corruption and the emergence of new corrupt practices, opportunities, unreasonable

---

[1] Anisimov, E. V. Imperial Russia. St. Petersburg, 2016. pp. 543–544.

concessions to foreign investors and foreign manufacturers at the expense of weakening customs protectionism and flirting with the persistent idea of "free trade," which was beneficial to English capital at the time.

"Abuses associated with entrepreneurial fever in the ministerial offices had reached such proportions that they attracted the attention of the Third Department" (1). The head of the Finance Minister's office, Kobeko, had a reputation as a notorious bribe-taker, while the stockbrokers **V. A. Poletika** and **I. A. Vyshnegradsky** were experienced bribe-givers. The latter cynically stated that "the treasury was created to be stolen from" (2).

The outrageous mistake of the ruling near liberal circles was the creation in 1857 of **the General Society of Russian Railways**, which "effectively obtained a monopoly on the construction of the most important railway lines (St. Petersburg–Warsaw, Moscow–Nizhny Novgorod, Orel–Kursk–Libava)" (3). The founders of the enterprise, with an estimated capital of 275 million rubles, were mainly Western bankers. The company received an insurance guarantee of 5% of the entire capital for 85 years.

Fig. 3.42. P. A. Valuev

Fig. 3.43. Grand Duchess Elena Pavlovna

---

¹ Laverichev, V. Ya. The Large Bourgeoisie in Post-Reform Russia. 1861–1900. Moscow, 1974. P. 48.

² Ibid. pp. 48–49.

³ Laverichev, V. Ya. The Large Bourgeoisie in Post-Reform Russia. 1861–1900. Moscow, 1974. P. 50.

Under the terms of the subscription, Russia was to receive only 37.5% of the capital, with 28.3%, 21%, and 1.2% going to England, France, and Prussia, respectively. However, in reality, all shares were actually placed in Russia. Foreign organizers limited themselves to speculative trading on the stock exchange and withdrew from the construction itself. At the same time, "all foreign railway orders were completely concentrated in the hands of the leaders of the Paris committee, the overwhelming majority of which were distributed among English metallurgical plants" (1).

By 1858, the company was already on the verge of bankruptcy. "The predatory management of international bankers led by Pereira, Stieglitz, Bering and Co., together with the Russian court camarilla, led the Main Society of Russian Railways to complete financial bankruptcy in the early 1860s, which caused the ruble to fall in Russia" (2).

Alexander II and his entourage were not solely responsible for the idealistic perception of the West and Western capital. A shameful page in the history of autocracy was the participation in the railway concession bacchanalia of the manager of the State Bank, E. N. Lamansky, the Minister of the Imperial Court, A. V. Adlerberg, and the Chairman of the Committee of Ministers, Prince P. P. Gagarin. "Alexander II, not disdaining millions in bribes, which went mainly into the pockets of his mercenary favorite, the illustrious Princess E. M. Dolgorukova-Yuryevskaya and her relatives, personally oversaw the distribution of railway concessions" (3).

***

In the 1860s and 1870s, the intensity of public debate between Slavophiles and Westernizers subsided, and the Slavophile movement itself began to transform into Pan-Slavism — the doctrine of solidarity among all Slavic peoples. Pan-Slavic elements were present in the 1840s, particularly in the work of the poet and entrepreneur **Fyodor Tyutchev** (1803–1873), who, while living abroad, took on the role of foreign policy propagandist for the empire. In his article "Russia and the Revolution" (1849), he states that in the

---

[1] Solovyova, A. M. Railway Transport in Russia in the Second Half of the 19th Century. Moscow, 1975. P. 71.

[2] Solovyova, A. M. Railway Transport in Russia in the Second Half of the 19th Century. Moscow, 1975. P. 73.

[3] Ibid. p. 105.

Fig. 3.44. F. I. Tyutchev   Fig. 3.45. M. P. Pogodin

modern world there are only two forces: revolutionary Europe and conservative Russia, which must unite the Slavic peoples. In another article, "The Papacy and the Roman Question" (1850), he expresses the opinion that the Revolution did not begin at the end of the 18th century in France or with the Reformation of the 16th century — it originated in the papacy, thanks to which the church became a vile institution. Tyutchev foresaw the Crimean War, which, as he wrote, was a conspiracy against Russia (1) (Fig. 3.44).

Tyutchev, who was quite optimistic in the 1840s and 1850s about the idea of uniting the Slavic peoples (including the Poles) after the Polish uprising of 1863–1864, was disappointed, seeing in these events "heroic fervor, betrayal, and lies." He believed that the rejection of Poland would violate the integrity of Russia, and this was precisely how it was perceived by the overwhelming majority of Russian public opinion (2).

The position of another early supporter of Pan-Slavism, **M. P. Pogodin** (1800–1875), a writer and historian who rejected the extremes of Slavophilism, was noteworthy. Pogodin was the son of a serf who gained his

---

[1] Labanov, S. Fyodor Tyutchev: poet, entrepreneur, political publicist (on the 200th anniversary of the birth of F. I. Tyutchev) // Internet magazine of the Sretensky Monastery. URL: https://pravoslavie.ru/jurnal/ 031216111111.htm (accessed: 22.02.2021).

[2] Shishkova N. M. F. I. Tyutchev's political poetry as part of his worldview // Bulletin of Adyghe State University. Series 2. Philology and Art Studies. 2013.№ 1. Pp. 54–60.

Fig. 3.46. N. Ya. Danilevsky

freedom, graduated from Moscow University, and became a writer and then a journalist. Together with S. P. Shevyrev, he published and edited the magazine "Moskvityanin" (1841–1856). After defending his master's thesis in 1825, he taught at Moscow University until 1844 (Fig. 3.45).

In the 1840s, Pogodin became fascinated with Pan-Slavic ideas and established contacts with the Czech philologists Šafařík and Palacký. By 1857, he had proposed to Alexander II that a Slavic Committee be organized, and after a became its chairman.

Pogodin's contribution as a public Figure was that he formulated the main differences between Russia and the West:

1) the important role of the state, in which its head is a protector rather than an enemy;

2) the position of vassals as an intermediate layer between the sovereign and the people, while in the West the disruptive formula "the vassal of my vassal is not my vassal" applies;

3) the existence of communal property under the authority of the prince, the sovereign, while in the West it belonged to the vassal.

M. P. Pogodin was an extremely popular publicist in the 1830s–1850s and was perceived as one of the "mouthpieces" of the official doctrine of nationality, close to Minister S. S. Uvarov, but he was largely forgotten in the post-reform period (1).

Meanwhile, the most prominent representative of Pan-Slavism in the 1870s was **Nikolai Yakovlevich Danilevsky** (1822–1885). The son of a general and a graduate of the Tsarskoye Selo Lyceum, he was an auditor at the Faculty of Natural Sciences of St. Petersburg University. In 1849, he was

---

[1] Teslya, A. "The Slavic Question" in the Journalism of M. P. Pogodin in the 1830s–1850s. // Sociological Review. 2014. Vol. 13, p№ 1. p. 118.

arrested in connection with the case of Petrashevsky, but after 100 days of imprisonment in the Peter and Paul Fortress, he was expelled from the capital. He served in the office of the governor of Vologda, then Samara. In 1853, he published a monumental book, The Climate of the Vologda Province. He then conducted research for the Department of Agriculture on the White Sea and the Arctic Ocean, the Caspian Sea, and the Sea of Azov (Fig. 3.46).

Danilevsky's main work, Russia and Europe, was published in 1871. In it, he put forward a theory of cultural-historical types as local ethno-civilizational communities. The scholar identified 10 fully developed types: Egyptian; Chinese; Assyrian-Babylonian-Phoenician; Indian; Iranian; Jewish; Greek; Roman; Arabian; Germanic-Romance (European). Russia forms a new Slavic civilizational community, which should manifest itself in the future, and it contrasts sharply with Europe. At the same time, Europe "sees in Russia and the Slavs in general something alien to it, and at the same time something that cannot serve as simple material from which it could derive benefits, as it does from China, India, Africa, most of America, etc., a material that could be shaped and molded in its own image and likeness..." (1).

In the third chapter of his work, Danilevsky rightly notes the conventionality of geographical boundaries, drawing attention to why the Ural Mountains should be considered the dividing line between Europe and Asia. At the same time, Russia has followed a completely different historical path than Europe. "It was not part of Charlemagne's renewed Roman Empire... it was not bound together into a single body by a feudal-aristocratic network... Russia also did not participate in the struggle against feudal violence, which led to the establishment of the form of civil liberty that this struggle had developed; it did not Fight against the oppression of a false form of Christianity (a product of lies, pride, and ignorance, glorifying itself as Catholicism) and has no need for the form of religious freedom called Protestantism... in a word, it is not involved in either European good or European evil..." (2).

Russia cannot be considered "adopted by Europe." Europe is ready to give Russia the role of being the bearer and disseminator of European civilization in the East, but it hinders the progress of the spread of Russian influence to Turkey, the Caucasus, Persia, China, and India.

---

[1] Danilevsky, N. Ya. Russia and Europe. Moscow, 2021. P. 76.

[2] Ibid. pp. 94–95.

According to the publicist, Russia does not dream of being part of the European political system. "...Russia is too big and powerful to be just one of the great European powers..." (1). The Pan-Slavic Union could be a counterweight to Europe.

This federation could include:

1) Russia with Galicia and Dobruja annexed to it;
2) The Kingdom of Serbs, Croats, and Slavs;
3) The Kingdom of Bulgaria;
4) The Kingdom of Romania;
5) The Kingdom of Greece (Crete, Cyprus, Epirus, Rhodes);
6) The Kingdom of Hungary (Hungary and Transylvania);
7) The Tsargrad District with its capital in Constantinople (2).

This plan was based on the division of the Austro-Hungarian Habsburg Monarchy and Turkey, carried out in the struggle against the European coalition led by France. It was assumed that Prussia would be Russia's ally.

Despite all the external appeal and emotional exaltation of the ideas of Pan-Slavism, they suffered from undoubted utopianism due to:

1) the unwillingness of the Western and Southern Slavic peoples, who were subject to expansion by the West and the Ottoman Empire, to show real solidarity with Russia;

2) the Russian Empire's lack of material and military resources to stand up to the West on the fate of the Slavs.

This situation was well understood by such an influential public Figure as **M. N. Katkov** (1818–1887), the son of a titular councilor and a graduate of Moscow University (1838), who became famous for his journalistic and publishing activities (Fig. 3.47). After five years of teaching at Moscow University, he became editor of the University Gazette (1851), and in 1856 he became editor of the Russian Herald, a leading scientific and literary monthly magazine that published works by I. S. Turgenev, L. N. Tolstoy, and F. M. Dostoevsky. Together with P. M. Leontiev, professor of Roman literature at Moscow University, he became the leaseholder of the newspaper "Moscow Vedomosti" (1863–1887), whose political course shifted from liberal to conservative and protective.

---

[1] Danilevsky, N. Ya. Russia and Europe. Moscow, 2021. p. 580.

[2] Ibid. pp. 561, 562.

Advocating for a strong state, the publicist believed that it made no sense for Russia to expand its borders and weaken itself by incorporating new Slavic territories. He considered Pan-Slavism dangerous not only for Austria-Hungary, which had absorbed the western and southern Slavic peoples, but also for Russia.

In the 1880s, the Russian Empire entered a post-liberal and then imperialist phase of its development. The deliberate revolution came to an end, and industrialization began in the 1890s. Economic development accelerated sharply, although its successes, given the enormous size of the territory, were enclave in nature (advanced industrial production flourished in St. Petersburg, Moscow and around Moscow, and in the Donbass).

Fig. 3.47. M. N. Katkov

The balance of socio-political forces and public opinion also changed. There was an increasingly complex differentiation of socio-political thought. The revolutionary wing grew stronger, now including not only the nobility and the gentry, but also workers' organizations. In Odessa in 1875, the South Russian Workers' Union was formed, and in St. Petersburg in 1878, the Northern Union of Russian Workers was formed. In Geneva in 1883, **G. V. Plekhanov** organized the group "Liberation of Labor." At the same time, several small circles led by D. I. Blagoev, N. E. Fedoseev, and M. I. Brusnev, consisting of students and intellectuals, were active in Russia.

Attempt to unite the scattered Marxist forces into the "Union for the Struggle for the Liberation of the Working Class" was undertaken in 1895 by V. I. Lenin and Y. O. Martov, but the formal establishment of the Russian Social Democratic Labour Party (RSDLP) took place only at the First Congress in Minsk in 1898. At the same time, the first populariser of Marxism in Russia, G. V. Plekhanov, adhered to the orthodox position on the impossibility of the country's transition to socialism without going

G. V. Plekhanov   V. I. Lenin   Y. O. Martov

Fig. 3.48. Founders of the "Union for the Struggle for the Liberation of the Working Class"

through the capitalist stage of development. V. I. Lenin took a more pragmatic position (Fig. 3.48).

Bolshevik thought "was unrestrained, reacted quickly to the emerging political situation, changed, and evolved" (1), and the Bolshevik Party itself skillfully used agitation among both workers and peasants.

The bourgeois-noble flank also became more active. With the emergence of the zemstvo system, the liberal-noble and bourgeois representatives gained practical experience and confidence in their own strengths.

These Figures began to claim power in the country, offering Western-style solutions.

A notable example in this regard is **P. N. Milyukov** (1859–1943), leader of the Cadet Party and a favorite of Western audiences (his lectures were greeted with cheers in the United States in 1903–1905) (2) (Fig. 3.49).

---

[1] History of Political and Legal Doctrines: Textbook for Universities. 2nd ed., stereotype / ed. by V. S. Nersesyants. Moscow, 1999. p. 622.

[2] Milyukov, P. N. Memoirs. Moscow, 1991. pp. 149–151, 172.

In 1906, in a private conversation with Prime Minister S. Yu. Witte, he advised, for tactical reasons and to save time, or Bulgaria (1). Another liberal, **P. B. Struve** (1870–1944), criticizing the national policy of imperial Russia, proposed adopting the more effective "organic hegemony" of the Anglo-Saxons in the United States and the British Empire (2). The Cadet Party was the most ambitious of all the centrist parties: at its peak (April 1906), it had 70,000 members, including representatives of the intelligentsia, merchants, petty bourgeoisie, liberal nobility, and even workers who had been deceived by bright slogans. The more moderate right-wing Union of October 17 had a similar membership during the 1905–1907 revolution (75,000 members, predominantly large industrialists and landowners), but unlike the Cadets, this organization fell apart in 1915. The Progressive Party, which was ideologically to the right of the Cadets but to the left of the Octobrists, attempted to forge a link between business and the intelligentsia.

In response to growing opposition in society, conservative and right-wing monarchist alliances emerged, but they were not inventive or constructive in their programs and did not have the necessary support of the masses.

The largest monarchist organization, the Union of the Russian People, enjoyed support mainly in provinces with a mixed national composition, and most of its members were Ukrainians, Belarusians, and Moldovans. Its possible membership (including sympathizers) was 330,000–400,000, which was clearly insufficient for political stabilization, and the most radical exceptions could not gain stable electoral support due to an underdeveloped political culture.

"No party had a majority in any province The situation was omplicated by the fact that it was not always clear who was right-wing and who was left-wing. The parties were not very popular among the public, even in 1906–1907" (Fig. 3.50).

According to rough estimates, at any given time after 1905, there were 10 right-wing, 12 centrist, and 5 left-wing parties in the country, not counting national parties.

---

[1] Leontovich, V. V. History of Liberalism in Russia. 1762–1914. Moscow, 1995. pp. 403–404.

[2] Struve, P. B. Patriotica. Politics, Culture, Religion, Socialism: A Collection of Articles from Five Years (1905–1910). St. Petersburg, 1911. p. 300.

| A. I. Guchkov — leader of the Octobrist Party | A. I. Konovalov — leader of the Progressive Party | A. I. Dubrovin — leader of the Union of the Russian People (until 1912) |

Fig. 3.50. Leaders of the major parties

The dangerous politicization of society could have been halted by the consolidation of Orthodox Christianity. Unfortunately, however, at the turn of the 19th and 20th centuries, there were virtually no outstanding Figures among the Orthodox clergy who were capable of inspiring the masses. One exception was **John of Kronstadt** (1820–1909), a preacher and spiritual writer who passed away shortly before World War I. He was the son of a priest in many generations. After graduating from the St. Petersburg Theological Academy in 1855, he was ordained a priest at St. Andrew's Cathedral in Kronstadt, where he served for 53 years until his death. At the same time, he taught God's Law at the local classical gymnasium for 25 years (Fig. 3.51).

Fig. 3.52. St. John's Stavropegial Convent

The bureaucratization and control of church life by the autocratic state naturally harmed the church and reduced its authority among the masses. However, there were notable exceptions. For example, **John of Kronstadt** proved to be a brilliant organizer of charity: through private donations and funds from monasteries, he managed to collect 40,000 rubles annually. On behalf of the Minister of Foreign Affairs, the idea of organizing workhouses was proposed to the governors for implementation. And yet, John gained even greater fame not as a philanthropist, but as a healer of souls. Thousands of pilgrims came to Kronstadt to participate in public healings. During his trips to cities across Russia, thousands and tens of thousands of people came to meet him.

He also had a reputation as a healer. Nowadays, many suffering people flock to his resting place in the St. John's Stavropegial Convent in St. Petersburg, where prayers to John of Kronstadt help them heal and solve their everyday problems (1) (Fig. 3.52). However, the clergyman's reputation during his lifetime was not so clear-cut. Along with his numerous supporters, who saw him as the embodiment of Jesus Christ (by the **Johannites**), there

---

[1] Modern miracles based on St. John of Kronstadt. URL: https://imonspb.ru/sv-prav-ioann-kronshtadtskiy/sovremennyie-chudesa-po-molitvam-sv-prav-ioanna-kronshtadtskogo/ (accessed: 07.05.2021).

were also sharp critics (primarily from liberal and Old Believer publications). John of Kronstadt expressed strong disapproval of the writer L. N. Tolstoy for his unorthodox views on religion. Politically, the clergyman stood for strict monarchism — he was one of the organizers of the Union of the Russian People.

Meanwhile, the appeal of the monarchist idea was waning, and with it, the influence of Orthodox Christianity, which was closely associated with it. Many extraordinary thinkers at the turn of the 19th and 20th centuries sensed this, although there was nothing they could do about it. The movement for the restoration of the conciliar principle in the governance of the Russian Orthodox Church was preached by **V. S. Solovyov** (1853– 1900) (Fig. 3.53). In particular, he wrote in 1881: "The council of the Russian Church must solemnly profess that the truth of Christ and his church do not need forced unity of forms and violent protection. By thus renouncing external police power, the church acquires internal moral authority, true power over souls and minds." (1)

Fig. 3.53. V. S. Solovyov

K. N. Leontiev (1831–1833) saw a socio-cultural perspective in "Byzantinism," whose features of which were autocracy, Orthodoxy, the collectivism of the peasant community, and conservatism (Fig. 3.54). It was he, and not the notorious "Slavism" was necessary for Russia's prosperity.

Fig. 3.54. K. N. Leontiev

---

[1] Solovyov V. S. On Spiritual Power in Russia // Collected Works. Vol. 3. St. Petersburg. P. 218.

He advocated isolation from the West even in everyday matters: "either not to dance at all, for example, but to pray to God, and if to dance, then in our own way, inventing or developing folk dance to exquisite refinement" (1).

In his work "The System of Russian State Power" (1912), advocated for distinctive state principles and autocracy, opposing the uncritical copying of Western legal experience.

Alas, the spiritual core of Russian civilization was broken during the 1905–1907 revolution and World War I. Russian society, as in the Time of Troubles at the beginning of the 17th century, was in disarray. It was saved from complete catastrophe by the October Revolution of 1917, which, at the cost of enormous sacrifices, brought a new system of social coordinates and a new ideology. The lesson to be remembered for the future is that it is not worth completely abandoning the old spiritual culture in the course of transformation. A renewed Orthodoxy and strong state power, implementing the idea of social justice, can and must serve the interests of the multi-ethnic Russian society.

The personality of the ruler is of great importance for the success of the state. It is difficult to accuse the Russian emperors of the 19th century of genius, but each of them, for better or worse, was in keeping with their historical era. **Alexander I,** known for his secretiveness, was able to impress with his outward liberalism and prevent social discontent from reaching extreme forms of expression. Let us remember that the Decembrist uprising took place after his reign. **Nicholas I,** distinguished by his military-bureaucratic pedantry, proved to be a very suitable Figure for overcoming the constitutional-political crisis in an authoritarian-acceptable form (only five participants in the Decembrist conspiracy received the highest punishment).

Alexander II, who earned the title of "Tsar-Liberator" from the liberals, opened up too much to the West and made inadequate foreign policy concessions.

Contrary to expectations of revolutionary turmoil in the 1880s, **Alexander III's** short reign turned out to be the most peaceful and stable. Despite the fact that Soviet historical science gave him unfavorable characteristics and accused him of "stupidity," **"primitive mind,"** and

---

[1] Leontiev, K. Selected Letters. St. Petersburg, 1993. P. 385.

"stubbornness," (1) his foreign and domestic policies, which avoided extremes and unnecessary conflicts, are noteworthy. He was a reformer by nature, but his good nature, **fairness, and at the same time firmness**, according to S. Yu. Witte, impressed those around him (2).

Alas, **Nicholas II** turned out to be the most inadequate of all rulers, while he faced systemic problems that had accumulated before him. The right wing, his main support, did not consider it possible to criticize him publicly, but privately "noted the impossibility of relying on the sovereign." He was reproached for his weakness and cowardice. "Dissatisfaction with his personal qualities was compounded by dissatisfaction with his entourage." (3)

There was a clear shortage of adequate statesmen around the monarch. The Chairman of the Council of Ministers, S. Yu. Witte (1849–1915), and P. A. Stolypin in 1905–1911 were lone Figures against the backdrop of an ineffective state machine, while the Minister of Finance, V. N. Kokovtsev (1853–1943), for all his abilities and prudence in matters of state finances, was only capable of maintaining the status quo as prime minister in 1911–1914, and nothing more (Fig. 3.55).

S. Y. Witte   P. A. Stolypin   V. N. Kokovtsev

Fig. 3.55. Prominent statesmen under Nicholas II

---

[1] Zayonchkovsky, P. A. Russian Autocracy at the End of the 19th Century (Political Reaction of the 1840s–Early 1890s). Moscow, 1970. pp. 35–46.

[2] Anisimov E. V. Imperial Russia... pp. 572–574.

[3] Lukyanov, M. N. Autocracy or Autocrat: Nicholas II through the Eyes of the Russian Right // Power. 2020.№ 7. pp. 160, 161.

The Figure of the pseudo-religious charlatan G. E. Rasputin, who clearly possessed certain hypnotic and extrasensory abilities, interfered in the process of state governance and distorted it, clearly discredited the ruling regime (1). His death in December 1916, shortly before the anti-monarchist revolution in February 1917, could do little to change the situation. It is characteristic that the right wing understood the futility of restoring the monarchy.

***

At the beginning of the 20th century, the configuration of the spiritual core of the Russian Empire was characterized by increased complexity and contradictions (Diagram 3.1). The cult of imperial autocracy, with its official and uninspiring formula of "Orthodoxy, autocracy, and nationality," had exhausted itself. The official, state-sanctioned Orthodox faith no longer enjoyed its former popularity: the extreme curtailment of church autonomy made clergy hostages to the population's negative attitude toward the state. The synthesis of Soviet patriotic thought and church faith could not radically change the situation, although Slavophilism and Pan-Slavism were, to a certain extent, a creative source for the development of Orthodoxy. On the other hand, Westernism, which had been flourishing since the mid-19th century, with its imposition of alien ideas on society, challenged both autocracy and Orthodoxy. The spread of the ideology of Enlightenment secularization and bourgeois rationality was another problem for the church.

The objective development of capitalism, combined with P. A. Stolypin's peasant reform, undermined centuries-old economic and social collectivism. The rigid structure of autocracy, established thanks to Peter I's Westernization, led to the loss of traditional conciliarity.

The activities of young and largely Western-oriented parties also did not contribute to the preservation of this form of socio-political collectivism. Until a certain point, the Russian Empire was preserved by the population's sense of imperialism and a certain administrative flexibility in relation to the national peripheries, but from the beginning of the 20th century, the authorities increasingly face nationalist challenges, and not only in Polish lands.

---

[1] Varfolomeev, Yu. V. G. E. Rasputin and the "Rasputin Affair" in the Fate of Russia at the Beginning of the 20th Century (based on materials from the Provisional Government's Extraordinary Investigation Commission) // News of Saratov University. Series: History and International Relations. 2011. Vol. 11, pNº 2. pp. 34–40.

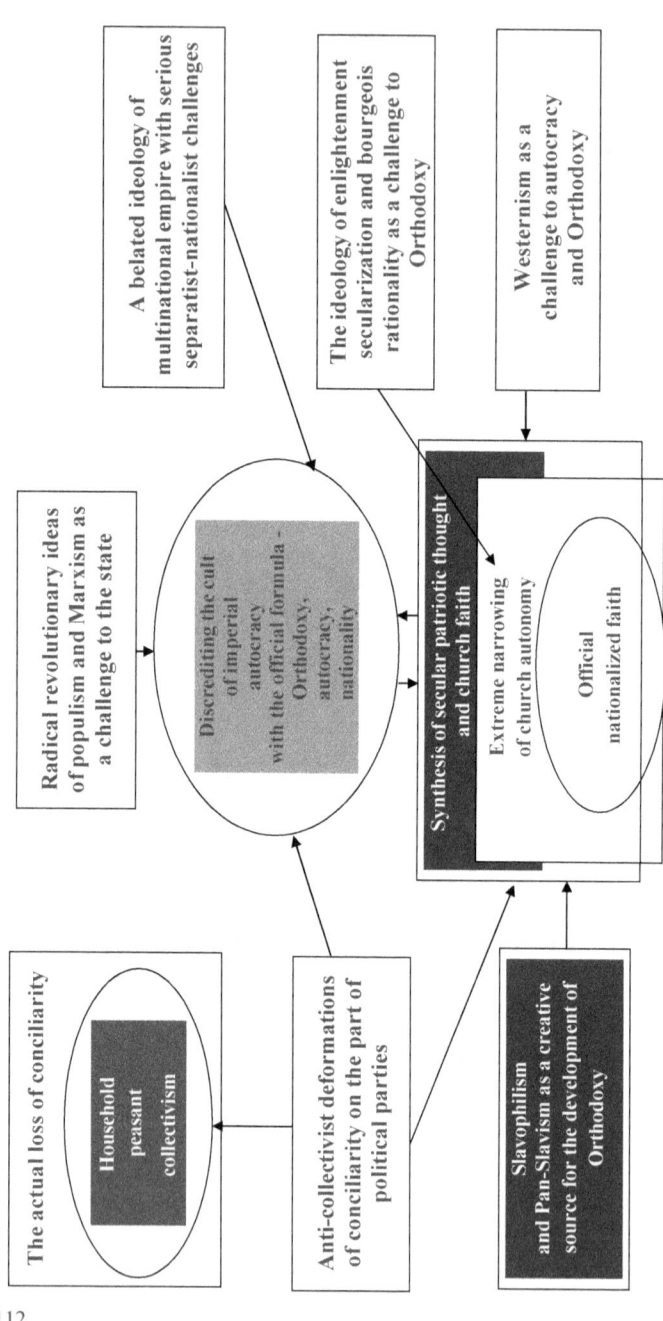

Diagram 3.1. The spiritual core of the Russian Empire at the turn of the 19th and 20th centuries.

However, radical revolutionary ideas still posed the greatest threat to the stability of society and the state. While populism demonstrated its official and political inexperience, Russian Marxism, seeking to take into account the social interests of both the peasantry and the proletariat, proved to be a more comprehensive force in its social activities. Of course, despite the numerous problems faced by the autocratic state at the beginning of the 20th century, it still had some opportunities to survive due to the well-known inertia of society, but then the First World War intervened, which was unnecessary and disastrous for tsarism and, in fact, destroyed its structure.

Essay 4
RADICALIZATION AND SUBSEQUENT STABILIZATION OF SPIRITUAL LIFE IN SOVIET AND POST-SOVIET RUSSIA

Judging by all appearances, social life develops cyclically, in a sharp clash of opposing tendencies. The inability of the former autocratic government to solve the acute problems gave rise to a nationwide crisis and two revolutions in 1917 during the exhausting First World War. It was these events that led the country to inevitable radicalization.

In accordance with the prevailing reality — the popularity of the idea of the Soviets in the mass consciousness — the Bolsheviks who came to power built a new socialist state as the Soviet Union. In doing so, they relied on Western ideas of Marxism, which were supplemented by the specific practice of state-building in a country that clearly did not belong to the West (Diagram 4.1).

Marxism-Leninism initially gravitated towards the idea of **proletarian internationalism,** which was highly controversial in terms of its practical implementation. The slogan "Workers of the world, unite!" implied that the victorious proletariat in a particular country should not put its own interests first, but rather the utopian ideal of a worldwide proletarian revolution. Of course, this slogan also had practical value — it could and did rally the proletariat of other countries to the defense of the victorious proletariat of a particular country. In the early years of Soviet power this was particularly important (1).

The First and Second Congresses of the Comintern (1919, 1920) — an organization designed to promote cooperation between the communist parties of different countries — were the culmination of the discussion of world revolution.

---

[1] Volkov, F. D. The Collapse of British Policy and the Diplomatic Isolation of the Soviet State (1917–1924). Moscow, 1954; Anti-war Traditions of the International Labor Movement. Moscow, 1972.

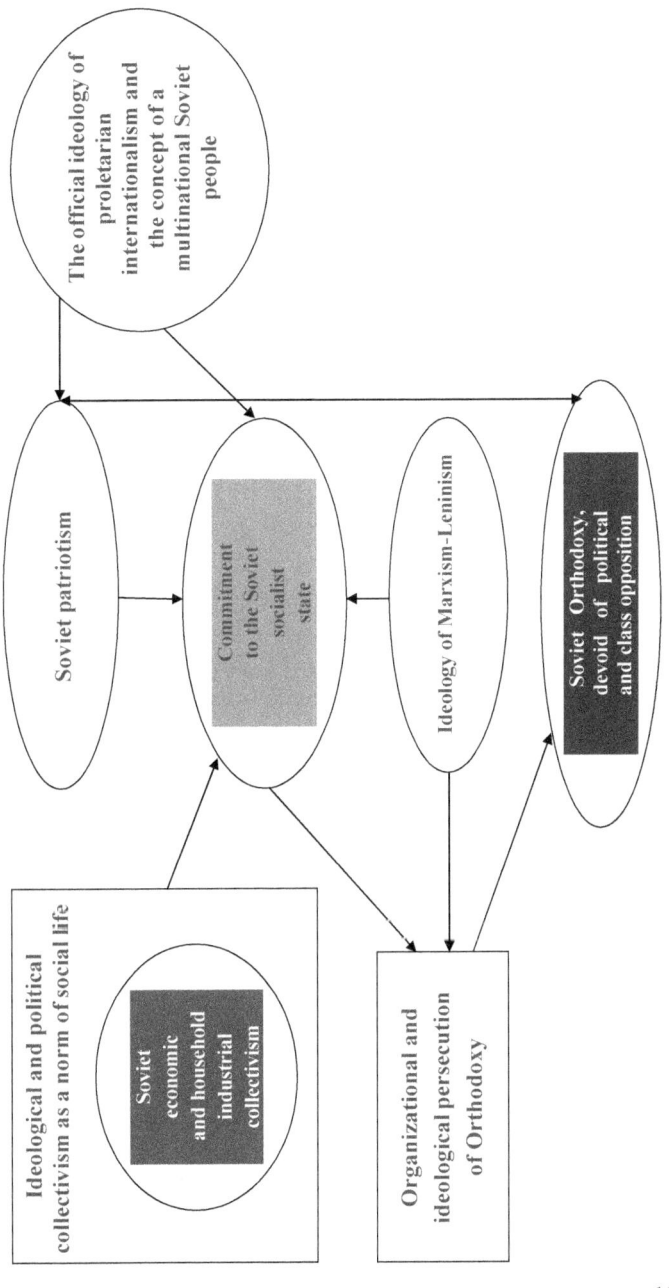

Diagram 4.1. The spiritual core of Soviet society and the state

They even won over representatives of the left-wing Social Democrats and put forward the slogan of a Federation of Soviet Republics of Europe and Asia (1). "...Attempts to "push" the belated proletarian revolution in the West were repeated in various forms until the mid-1920s. Thus, in 1923, measures were taken to carry out a socialist revolution in Germany, Poland, Bulgaria, and Italy, and in 1924 in Estonia." (2)

However, over time, the sense of the usefulness and realism of the idea of a world revolution began to weaken. True, at the declarative level, "the class approach and proletarian internationalism remained the basis of the USSR's foreign policy." In reality, however, "foreign policy was increasingly based on the national interests of the Soviet Union." (3) The course towards building socialism in one country, taken in the mid-1920s, was accompanied by the establishment of strict hegemony in the Comintern and a well-known reorientation towards preparing for revolutions in the countries of the East. From the mid-1930s, there was an official rejection of the idea of world revolutionary hegemony, and in 1943, an attempt was made to the dissolution of the Comintern (4).

After World War II, the idea of proletarian internationalism was put into practice through large-scale economic and military-political aid to socialist and developing countries. However, this aid was quite costly and not always effective, as it was spread across different continents. For example, according to rough estimates, the total debt of socialist countries in interest alone amounted to 1.3 billion rubles by 1960. Also, "from 1955 to 1965, the Soviet leadership, in addition to socialist countries, provided loans to 31 other states for a total amount of 7.3 billion rubles, of which 4.4 billion rubles were for economic purposes and 2.9 billion rubles were for the payment of military-technical property. At the same time, about 90% of all loans were granted to the following countries:

---

[1] Emelyanova, E. N. The Problem of War and Peace in the Context of the History of the Comintern (1919–1922). // Vlast. 2019. No. 1. Pp. 224–226.

[2] Panarin, A. A. Implementation of the Bolshevik Party's plans for a world socialist revolution in 1917–1920 // Humanities and Legal Studies. 2017.№ 2. P. 113.

[3] Gerishtein, I. Z. The factor of messianism in the foreign policy of the USSR // Bulletin of Vyatka State University of Humanities. 2017.№ 4. P. 54.

[4] Khudoley K. K. The evolution of ideas of world revolution in the politics of the Soviet Union (the era of the Comintern and socialism in one country) // Bulletin of St. Petersburg State University. Political Science. International Relations. 2017. Vol. 10, No. 2. P. 151–159.

UAR – 2 billion rubles, India – 1.6 billion rubles, Indonesia – 1.1 billion rubles, Afghanistan – 0.4 billion rubles, Iraq – 0.3 billion rubles, Algeria – 0.3 billion rubles, Syria – 0.3 billion rubles, Iran — 0.3 billion rubles. At the same time, loans were provided in free form and were usually repaid in national currency. Some repaid them with goods, often "unable to pay the USSR interest on the debt. The Soviet leadership granted deferrals or wrote off the debt" (1).

The concept of a multinational Soviet people proved to be more fruitful for the new regime. It was formed gradually, as Soviet federalism matured. The first national-territorial entities after the collapse of the Russian Empire emerged in the spring of 1918, and their development took place with the guidance and coordination of the People's Commissariat for Nationalities. Then, during the Civil War, a military alliance of republics was formed, and after its end, agreements on joint activities were concluded. Finally, in the second half of 1922, the process of concluding a federal treaty began, accompanied by unprecedented communication activity (2).

The establishment of the USSR initiated ethno-political integration against the backdrop of real material, organizational, and cultural assistance to the former national outskirts of the Russian Empire. However, in implementing national **policy,** it was necessary to deal with both objective difficulties (for example, the scattered settlement of nationalities, which made their territorial and administrative registration difficult and subjective (3), purely nationalistic deviations of individual ethnic elites and their representatives. In particular, the most dangerous nationalist tendencies in the 1920s and 1930s were **Sultan-Galiyevism,** with its idea of organizing Muslim federations in European Russia, Central Asia, the North Caucasus, and the Transcaucasus (4) and **Ukrainian nationalism.** The Bolsheviks quickly dealt with the Tatar tendency, but flirting with Ukrainian nationalism **(including the**

---

[1] Pivovarov, N. Yu., and Dzhamilov, T. A. Soviet Foreign Economic Strategy: Departmental Projects and Bureaucratic Mechanisms (Late 1950s–First Half of the 1960s) // New Historical Herald. 2019. № 4. Pp. 60, 61.

[2] Yakubovskaya S. I. The Development of the USSR as a Union State (1922–1936). Moscow, 1972. pp. 22–24.

[3] Administrative-Territorial Structure of Russia. Moscow, 2002. P. 210.

[4] Vdovin, A. I. The USSR: History of a Great Power (1922–1991). Moscow, 2019. p. 38.

forced imposition of the Ukrainian language) continued for quite a long time (1).

One way or another, the multinational Soviet people passed the test during the Great Patriotic War. There were only isolated cases of national separatism and disloyalty to the USSR, primarily in Ukraine (2). In the post-war period, the success of the integration processes was evidenced by the high geographical mobility of nationalities (for example, at the end of the 1950s, 44.3% of Armenians, 24.8% of Tajiks, 22.8% of Kazakhs, 17.5% of Belarusians, and 13.7% of Ukrainians lived outside their republics) % of Armenians, 24.8% of Tajiks, 22.8% of Kazakhs, 17.5% of Belarusians, and 13.7% of Ukrainians lived outside their republics) (3), and the number of interethnic marriages was also significant. As a result, the Soviet people, as a rigid ideological construct, entered official propaganda in the 1960s and 1970s.

Fig. 4.1. M. N. Pokrovsky (1868–1932)

The concept **of Soviet patriotism** began to be cultivated mainly in the 1930s, when it became clear that abstract and timeless class ideas, without reference to a specific state and society, were insufficient. Unfortunately, in the 1920s, the Bolsheviks were greatly influenced by the "historical school" of M. N. Pokrovsky (1868–1932) (Fig. 4.1), who held the post of Deputy People's Commissar of Education and enjoyed the patronage of prominent Bolshevik leaders of an anti-patriotic orientation — N. I. Bukharin, G. E. Zinoviev, and L. D. Trotsky (4). In his works, the Bolshevik historian interpreted Russian history from a vulgar class perspective, writing that the development of technology was allegedly determined by the class structure of society. He asserted the idea of the irrelevance of historical Figures, regarding them as agents of "commercial capital."

---

[1] Medvedev, A. The True History of the Russian and Ukrainian Peoples. Moscow, 2015. pp. 423–431.

[2] Cherkasov, A. A., Krinco, E. F., Shmigel, M. Ukrainian Nationalism During World War II: Nature and Manifestations // Rusin. 2015. No. 2.

[3] Zlatopolsky, D. L. The USSR — A Federal State. Moscow, 1967. P. 320.

[4] Spitsyn, E. Yu. Russia — Soviet Union. 1917–1945. Book III. Moscow, 2021. P. 191.

He emphasized the negative aspects of Russian history: wars of conquest, "colonial plundering of peoples."

After Pokrovsky's death, his supporters were accused, not without reason, of "anti-patriotism" and excessive "sociologism."

The state is taking steps to teach history in schools and write adequate textbooks. A new generation of historians — B. D. Grekov and E. V. Tarle — are studying history more seriously, relying on historical sources and adopting a benevolent approach (Figs. 4.2, 4.3). B. D. Grekov publishes his famous works on pre-Mongol Rus and the enslavement of the peasantry. E. V. Tarle, a brilliant popularizer of science, creates his patriotic-oriented works "Napoleon's Invasion of Russia" (1937), "The Crimean War" (Vol. 1–2, 1941–1943), Nakhimov (1944), and The Northern War and the Swedish Invasion of Russia (1958).

Fig. 4.2. B. D. Grekov (1882–1953)

In the spiritual life of Soviet society in the 1920s and 1930s, national separatism, and above all **Ukrainian nationalism**, were dangerous deformations. During the Civil War, it was in Ukraine that the most complex military operations took place, with clashes between the White movement, the Bolsheviks, and Ukrainian nationalists. nationalists (such as S. Petliura) and anarchist Makhnovism. At the same time, Ukraine suffers from an excess of weapons left behind by the German occupiers in 1918. In this situation, seeking to ease the situation, the Bolsheviks **make maximum concessions to Ukrainian** nationalism.

Fig. 4.3. E. V. Tarle (1874–1955)

In 1920, compulsory study of the Ukrainian language was introduced, and in 1923, a decision was made on "indigenization" — "that is, in essence, the forced reformatting of Russian or Little Russian identity into Ukrainian with the help of the party apparatus.

... In addition to schools, theaters, newspapers, universities, and civil servants who did not master the Ukrainian language were Ukrainianized and dismissed without the right to reinstatement... (1) And this despite the fact that, objectively speaking, Ukrainian identity has never been popular among either the masses or the elites! It is known that "for every 10,000 inhabitants of Ukraine, there were 155 Jewish communists, 88 Great Russian communists, and only 39 Ukrainian communists." (2).

However, Ukrainian nationalists became the instruments of ethnic violence: writer and historian M. S. Hrushevsky, who was appointed President of the Ukrainian Academy of Sciences, postulated the ideas of fundamental differences in the development of the Ukrainian and Russian peoples, and the negative influence of the consolidation of Russian lands from Ivan III to Catherine II. The People's Commissar of Education, Secretary of the Central Committee of the Communist Party of Ukraine V. P. Zatonsky, and the People's Commissar of Justice, Prosecutor General, and then People's Commissar of Education of Ukraine N. A. Skrypnyk, as high-ranking bureaucrats, were the leaders of Ukrainization. Poet and prose writer M. Khvylovy, author of the slogans "Away from Moscow" and "Orientation towards psychological Europe," persistently promoted the idea of competition between Russian and Ukrainian societies and saw the promotion of Russian culture in Ukraine as a "counterrevolutionary idea" (Fig. 4.4).

It was only in the early 1930s that the country's leadership changed its political course. "Indigenization was increasingly at odds with the trend toward greater centralization of state power that emerged in the 1930s. In addition, the authorities began to fear that continuing this policy could lead to a rise in local nationalism and separatism" (3). However, the seeds of national separatism had already been sown. Moreover, Ukrainization was sharply curtailed in the territories bordering Ukraine and in the lands within the RSFSR that historically belonged to Sloboda Ukraine, Novorossiya, and Kuban, but in Ukraine it was encouraged with reservations by the republic's top officials (4).

---

[1] Medvedev, A. The True History of the Russian and Ukrainian Peoples. Moscow, 2015. p. 419.

[2] Allen, E. D. History of Ukraine. The South Russian Lands from the First Kiev Princes to Joseph Stalin. Moscow, 2017. pp. 374–375.

[3] Isaev, V. I. The Turn in Soviet National Policy in the Mid-to-Late 1930s. // Peoples and Religions. Moscow, 2018. P. 101.

[4] Marchukov, A. V. Novorossiya. The Formation of National Identities (18th–20th Centuries). Moscow, 2018. pp. 357–359.

M. S. Hrushevsky (1866–1934)

V. P. Zatonsky (1888–1938)

N. A. Skrypnyk (1872–1933)

M. Khvylovy (1893–1933)

Fig. 4.4. Supporters of Ukrainization

In the process of building a new state and society, the old Russian, predominantly peasant-communal collectivism was transformed into **Soviet collectivism**. First and foremost, this collectivism had a productive basis: without collective unity, it was impossible to achieve success in the mobilization economy, in the rapid implementation of industrialization and collectivization. "On the one hand, the communist regime destroyed the traditional way of life in order to create a 'new man' adapted to the Soviet model of industrial civilization. On the other hand, the Soviet government, in instilling its own motivation for labor into the mass consciousness, relied on the traditional values of collectivism, spirituality (transformed into communist ideology and socialist consciousness), egalitarian justice, patience. " (1).

However, Soviet collectivism also had a domestic expression. "Communal homes were supposed to embody the idea of collective living. " (2) "Parades, physical culture parades, mass celebrations — the formation of a collective body also took place during festive times..." (3). But most importantly, ideological and political collectivism became the norm in public life, which was realized in mass campaigns (electoral, party, trade union, and Komsomol).

Under the new social order, **the position of Orthodox Christianity changed radically**. Based on Marxist postulates, "revolutionary expediency," and the clergy's not always loyal attitude toward it, the Soviet government waged a struggle against religion. At the time of the October Revolution of 1917, the Orthodox Church, freed from the strict control of the autocracy, began a certain organizational restructuring. There was a series of resignations of compromised hierarchs (for example, the bishops of St. Petersburg and Moscow, Makarii and Pitirim, who were supporters of G. Rasputin). " of the nearly 150 years of pre-revolutionary bishops, about forty bishops were removed from their **sees** (1). The new chief prosecutor of the Synod, V. N. Lvov, initiated a radical overhaul of this unelected body and set about preparing

---

[1] Kutkovets, T. I., Klyamkin, I. M. Russian and Western Workers // Vedomosti Prikladnoy Etiki. 2000. № 17. P. 72.

[2] Lebina N. B. Soviet Everyday Life: Norms and Anomalies. From War Communism to the High Life. Moscow, 2015. P. 78.

[3] Ovodova S. N. Soviet Socialism and Physical Collectivism: Practices of Transforming Everyday Life // Man in the World of Culture. 2017. No. 4. P. 58.

for **an All-Russian Local Council** and establishing a **Pre-Council Council** (Fig. 4.5).

In the course of this work, the principle of election was widely established in the church organization, both with regard to bishops and monasteries. Political differentiation was observed among the clergy and laity: for example, **the All-Russian Union of Democratic Orthodox Clergy and Laity,** which emerged in March 1917, clearly held left-wing views, enjoyed the support of the Provisional Government, and put forward Socialist Revolutionary slogans.

Fig. 4.5. V. N. Lvov (1872–1930)
Chief Prosecutor of the Synod

Other organizations were also created, such as **the Union of Progressive Clergy**, which attempted to engage with workers, and **the Christian Social Workers' Party**. However, "the majority of the clergy was generally apolitical and, while advocating democratic reforms in the structure of the Church, did not share the demands of the socialist parties for its separation from the state" (2). This idea was also enshrined in the document of the Pre-Council Council of July 13, 1917: in particular, "it spoke of the need for the Church to be independent of the state, but to retain its basic former rights, including state appropriations" (3).

The All-Russian Local Council, which opened in Moscow on August 15, 1917, brought together 564 delegates, including 80 bishops, representatives of monasteries, 163 members of the white clergy, and 299 lay people. **The lay people played an important role in consolidating the council** and overcoming long-standing contradictions between the clergy and the population. There was obvious "mutual distrust between the clergy and representatives of educated society." "On the other hand, for all groups of lay people, including the peasant population, was dissatisfied with the fact that the lion's share of parish

---

[1] Shkarovsky, M. V. The Russian Orthodox Church in the 20th Century. Moscow, 2010. P. 62.

[2] Ibid. p. 67.

[3] Ibid. p. 68.

Fig. 4.6. Patriarch Tikhon (Belavin) (1865–1925)

income went to maintain religious educational institutions — which were class-based in their structure, that is, in fact, to the class needs of the clergy. In addition, "the line of division ran between the white and black, monastic clergy... Parish priests believed that the monastics were in a privileged position, that they had 'seized power' in the church..." Finally, discontent was also building up in connection with the unequal material support provided to those holding higher and lower spiritual positions. The junior ones, "who did not have the sacred rank of psalm readers, felt their social and material real inferiority compared to priests. At the same time the rural clergy felt humiliated in front of the urban clergy, the provincial clergy in front of the metropolitan clergy, and so on." (1)

The main achievement of the first session of the Council, held in August-December 1917, was **the restoration of the patriarchate** and the election of Metropolitan **Tikhon** (Belavin) of Moscow as Patriarch (1865–1925), who had considerable experience in church service as Bishop of Lublin, Bishop of Aleutian and North American, head of the Yaroslavl and Rostov dioceses, and Archbishop of Vilnius, who was elected in June 1917 as the ruling archbishop of Moscow (Fig. 4.6). At the same time, the participants of the council had to respond to the first acts of the Soviet government, the seriousness of which they initially underestimated. The Council document of December 2, 1917 ("On the Legal Status of the Orthodox Russian Church") provided for the separation, but not the separation, of the church from the state, but most of its articles were unrealistic. "Until the end of 1917, the church leadership believed that Soviet power was unstable and weak, and therefore, fearing the wrath of the believing people, it will not take decisive action...".

---

[1] Beglov, A. The All-Russian Church Council of 1917–1918 as a phenomenon of the Church's conciliar practice // State, Religion, Church in Russia and Abroad. 2016. No. 1. Pp. 57–58.

For example, the Decree on Land, which provided for the nationalization of church and monastery lands, "was considered by the conciliar majority... as a declaration without any real basis..." (1). The same approach was taken in assessing the People's Commissariat of Education's decision to transfer all religious educational institutions to its control and the decrees on civil marriage and civil registration.

In January 1918, the mood among the hierarchs and participants of the Council changed, as a draft decree was published on December 31, 1917, and on January 23, 1918, **the Council of People's Commissars issued a decree "On the Separation of Church and State and School and Church."** "Its rejection was exacerbated by the fact that local authorities often interpreted it in the worst possible way for the clergy. Priests were often arrested not for counterrevolutionary agitation, but for their unwillingness to assist commissions in inventorying church property..." (2). Patriarch Tikhon himself, in his appeal of January 19, 1918, could not resist exacerbating relations: he branded the enemies of Christ's Truth and excommunicated them, although he did not directly mention the Soviet government.

At the same time, there was a noticeable growth in religious sentiment, including among the peasantry. "While they generally supported the expropriation of church and monastery property, they reacted negatively to the introduction of civil registration, the deprivation of property rights, and the removal of the Law of God from schools." (3)

In the atmosphere of revolutionary activism within Orthodoxy, **the renewal movement** was gaining strength. One of its leaders was Father **Alexander Vvedensky** (1889–1946). The son of a gymnasium director from Vitebsk and a graduate of the History and Philology Faculty of St. Petersburg University, he became close to representatives of the God-seeking intelligentsia in his youth and was ordained a priest in 1914. After February 1917, his service as a regimental priest in the army and a priest at the Cavalry School was replaced by political activity and rapprochement with the Socialist Revolutionaries.

Vvedensky is the author of numerous articles and pamphlets and is best known for his disputes with militant atheists, with traditionalist clergymen.

---

[1] Kashevarov, A. N. Development of the official position of the Orthodox Church regarding Soviet power and its religious policy at the Local Council of 1917–1918 // Bulletin of St. Petersburg University. Ser. 2. 2007. № 2. P. 50.

[2] Shkarovsky, M. V. The Russian Orthodox Church in the 20th Century... p. 76.

[3] Ibid. p. 78.

At the same time, he is a serious analyst who, in his most famous work, showed the objective difficulties that arose in Orthodoxy after February 1917. "The Church was the stronghold of the monarchy," notes Vvedensky. "When the monarchy collapsed, the church was left hanging in the air And so, in the spring of 1917, the church was in turmoil. The best (not very numerous) forces of the church want to establish friendly, rather than hostile, relations with the liberated people. But there is a strong, gloomy reaction within the church. It is lying low. But soon it will raise its head. As the revolution develops, all reactionary forces are rallying **around the church."** (1)

Vvedensky himself had rather unusual views on matters of faith. "For him, everything in the world is an intersection of currents and impulses Life impulses seem to receive orders from the center, like cells in the human body. God is, therefore, both the Divine Number (the Trinity) and the Center from which impulses emanate. **Christ is the manifestation of the Supreme Impulse. In him is Truth, Life, and Beauty."** (2)

Vvedensky was the most prominent and charismatic representative of the diverse Renovationist movement. At the same time, its most honest and sincere member was **Alexander Ivanovich Boyarsky** (1885–1937) — a "working priest" who enjoyed enormous popularity among the workers of the Izhora factory in **Kolpino. V. D. Krasnitsky** (1881–1936), the de facto leader of the Renovationist movement in its early months, can be described as an outright scoundrel and informer associated with the OGPU. More complex is the mindset of **S. V. Kalinovsky** (1884–1930), the son of a hereditary nobleman, who was considered a "Bolshevik" among his comrades, took holy orders in 1923, and became a mediocre atheist lecturer. Finally, **Bishop Antonin (Granovsky)** (1865–1927) was considered an outstanding expert in ancient languages. He was dismissed in January 1917 due to illness from his post as Bishop of Vladikavkaz and Mozdok and became close to the Bolsheviks in the Committee for Aid to the Starving. From May 1922 to June 1923, he was chairman of the Higher Church Administration, the governing body of the Renovationist Church (Fig. 4.7).

---

[1] Archpriest A. Vvedensky. Church and State. Moscow, 1923. P. 3.

[2] Krasnov-Levitin, A. Works and Days: The Renovationist Metropolitan Alexander Vvedensky. Paris, 1990. p. 41.

Alexander Ivanovich Vvedensky (1889–1946) was one of the leaders of the Renovationist Church.

Alexander Ivanovich Boyarsky (1885–1937)

Vladimir Dmitrievich Krasnitsky (1881–1936)

Sergei Kalinovsky (1884–1930)

Antonin Granovsky (1865–1927)

Fig. 4.7. Leaders of the Renovationist movement

The newest church organization, as an alternative to traditional Orthodoxy, was established by the Soviet authorities at a time when relations between the secular and ecclesiastical authorities had once again become strained. This time, the reason was the implementation of the All-Russian Central Executive Committee's decree of February 23, 1922, on the confiscation of church property not directly related to the practice of religion and its transfer to the needs of the starving. The authorities regarded the ensuing unrest among the faithful as instigated by the clergy and began interrogating Patriarch Tikhon, who was placed under house arrest. It was at this moment, on May 12, 1922, that A. I. Vvedensky, together with other clergymen, visited the patriarch and insisted that he temporarily relinquish his powers and transfer them to Metropolitan Agafangel. Later, on May 16, they formed **the Supreme Church Administration (SCA)**, headed by Bishop Antonin, who was elevated to the rank of metropolitan.

Initially, the organization of a new, reformist church structure, accompanied by the disorganization of the old structure, was successful: in 1922–1923, more than half of the Russian episcopate and parishes came under the wing of the reformists. However, Patriarch Tikhon's release from prison and the beginning of disagreements within the reformist camp prompted him to reorganize it into the Holy Synod of the Russian Orthodox Church. The chairmen of the board were successively Metropolitan **Evdokim (Meshchersky)** of Odessa in 1923–1924, Metropolitan **Veniamin (Muratovsky)** in 1925–1930, and Metropolitan Archbishop **Vitaly (Vvedensky)** of Tula and Epifan **in** 1930–1935. The same Metropolitan Vitaly, in connection with the abolition of the Synod in 1935, was proclaimed First Hierarch of Moscow and of all Orthodox Churches in the USSR. The last head of the renewal organization was Alexander Vvedensky in 1941–1945, and at the end of the Great Patriotic War, Joseph Stalin made the final decision that an alternative church organization was unnecessary.

Meanwhile, traditional Orthodoxy gradually regained its position. After the death of Patriarch Tikhon in 1925 and the arrest of his successors in 1927, **Metropolitan Sergius (Stragorodsky)**, who took a more loyal position towards the Soviet authorities, became the locum tenens of the patriarchal throne (1).

---

[1] Safonov, D. V. The Activities of Metropolitan Sergius (Stragorodsky) in the Context of Soviet Religious Policy in 1921–1926 // Bulletin of Chelyabinsk State University. History. 2009.№ 23. Issue 33. Pp. 58–66.

In July 1927, he issued a declaration in which he defined his attitude toward the state as follows: "We want to be Orthodox Christians and at the same time recognize the Soviet Union as our civil homeland, whose joys and successes are ours, and whose failures are our failures." (1)

Many accused and continue **to accuse Metropolitan Sergius of "painting himself in Soviet colors," "weak-willedness," "politicking," renouncing "church freedom," and "compromising with reforms."** (2) However, this was a wise position based on centuries-old tradition "symphony of powers" and non-resistance to the Soviet state. As a result, "the Church preserved the most important thing — its existence in Russia and its spiritual and moral significance in the hearts of believers. The state realized that it could not destroy either the Church or **Orthodoxy."** (3) In this regard, the 1930s, the Soviet authorities shifted from direct organizational attacks on clergy to indirect pressure on the spiritual and religious sphere of citizens.

In particular, the activities of the Union of Militant Atheists, headed by **E. M. Yaroslavsky** (1878–1943), the Bolshevik Party's chief expert on religious issues and editor of the newspaper Bezbozhnik and the magazines Bezbozhny Krokodil (The Godless Crocodile), Bezbozhnik u Stanka (The Godless Man at the Machine), Bezbozhnik (The Godless Man), and author of primitive atheistic works.

The level of these publications is well characterized by some of their covers: for example, the title page of Bezbozhnik u stanka for 1929 No. 15, workers are depicted carrying Jesus Christ away in a wheelbarrow, and the cover of the November 1930 issue contains an image of a swastika, a dollar sign, and a Bible with a cross.

The church was not spared the "Great Terror" of the late 1930s: in this respect, it shared the fate of the entire country. According to some estimates, in the 1930s and 1940s, about 45 thousand clergymen were arrested or **liquidated** (4).

---

[1] The Russian Orthodox Church in Soviet Times. Book 1. Moscow, 1995. P. 270.

[2] Mazyrin, A. V. On the Question of the "Renovationist Nature of Sergianism" // Bulletin of the Russian Orthodox Church. Series II History. History of the Russian Orthodox Church. 2015. № 2 (63). Pp. 84–98.

[3] Zagrebin S. S. Power and the Renovationist Schism in the Russian Orthodox Church // Society and Power. 2009. № 3. P. 15.

[4] Pospelovsky D. V. The Russian Orthodox Church in the 20th Century. Moscow, 1995. P. 176.

By 1939, throughout the country less than 100 of the 60,000 churches that existed in 1917 remained active. (1) However, during the critical period of the Great Patriotic War for the country and society, the state and the Church managed to find a compromise. Already in the first months of the war, the authorities began to curtail anti-religious propaganda. In turn, clergymen participated in patriotic education and the defense of the country through their words and deeds: by the summer of 1945, more than 300 million rubles had been collected for the needs of the front, not counting jewelry, clothing, and food (2). At a turning point in the Great Patriotic War, in September 1943, Joseph Stalin met with three Orthodox hierarchs: Metropolitan Sergius, Metropolitan Alexius of Leningrad, and Metropolitan Nicholas of Kiev. During the meeting, issues were raised concerning the opening of churches and new parishes, the restoration of church educational institutions, and the publication of a printed organ. But most importantly, a council of 19 bishops was soon held, which elected Sergius as patriarch and determined the composition of the Synod (Fig. 4.8). At the end of the war, from January 31 to February 4, 1945, after Sergius' death in May 1944, **a more representative Local Council** was held**,** which elected **Metropolitan Alexius of Leningrad** (Simansky) (1877–1970) as the new patriarch (Fig. 4.9). The same council also approved new **Regulation about the leadership of the Russian Orthodox Church**.

Patriarch Alexy I came from a noble family (a descendant of the Rurikids), received a fundamental secular education at the law faculty of Moscow University, and then graduated from the Moscow Theological Academy. He was a bishop, the first vicar of the Novgorod diocese, when the October Revolution of 1917 happened. During the Soviet era, he was arrested a bunch of times, spoke out against the Renovationist movement, and was a close associate of Patriarch Sergius. In fact, it was under him that the reopening of churches began (in 1944 and the first half of 1945, 414 out of 5 770 applications were **approved)** (3). **The** Russian Orthodox Church began to establish international contacts.

---

[1] Zelenova, O. V. The Russian Orthodox Church during the Great Patriotic War. URL: https://pravednik.info/russkaya-pravoslavnaya-cerkov-v-gody-velikoj-otechestvennoj-vojny.html (accessed: 20.05.2022).

[2] Vasilyeva O. Yu. The Russian Orthodox Church in 1927–1943 // Questions of History. 1994. No. 4.

[3] Morozova E. N. State Power, the Russian Orthodox Church, and Society during the Great Patriotic War // Bulletin of the St. Petersburg University of the Ministry of Internal Affairs of Russia. 2005. No. 2 (26). P. 52.

Fig. 4.8. Locum tenens of the patriarchal throne, Patriarch Sergius

Fig. 4.9. Patriarch Alexy

However, the period of normalization of state-church relations lasted only a decade and a half, and it was interrupted primarily by political circumstances. The new Soviet leader, Nikita Khrushchev, known for his voluntarism and ill-conceived pseudo-populist policies, after his final victory in the internal political struggle in 1957, considered it extremely advantageous to continue the course of "de-Stalinization." Tightening the policy towards Orthodox Christianity "would not shake the foundations of the political system and could not even cause noticeable rejection among Stalinists." In addition, in light of the notorious slogan about the imminent "victory of communism," it was necessary to demonstrate "successes." "It was believed that religion and the church would be easier to deal with than, say, the creation of a society of complete abundance or the elimination of differences between city and village, mental and physical labor" (1).

---

[1] Soskovets, L. I. The Position of the Russian Orthodox Church during the "Khrushchev Thaw" // Bulletin of Tomsk State University. History. 2011. No. 4 (16). Pp. 29, 30.

The persecution of the church began with the publication in October 1958 of two decrees by the Council of Ministers of the USSR: "On Monasteries in the USSR" and "On Increasing Taxes on the Income of Diocesan Enterprises and Monasteries." In November 1958, another document was published: "On Measures to Stop Pilgrimages to So-Called Holy Places." The authorities had several goals in mind, including reducing the economic and human resources of the church, decreasing the number of parishes and monasteries, and eliminating the institution of pilgrimage.

It must be said that the initiators of the anti-religious political war achieved a great deal. The number of clergymen decreased almost twice between 1958 and 1964 (from 12 169 to 7 673), and the number of churches and houses of prayer decreased by about the same amount (from 13 324 to 7 873) (1).

They managed to close down the theological seminaries in Kyiv, Stavropol, Saratov, Minsk, and Volyn, so that by the mid-1960s, only three such educational institutions remained, and the number of seminarians had decreased by 44 times. (2) However, the economic base of the Church and the level of religiosity proved to be more difficult. Despite the fact that in the first half of the 1960s, anti-church pressure intensified and new restrictions were imposed, even in areas with the highest anti-church activity, the effectiveness of the measures taken was questionable. Thus, "in the Ternopil region, the number of churches decreased from 804 to 541, the number of baptisms decreased from 12 711 to only 12 673, while revenues increased from 332 000 rubles to 503 000 rubles; in the Dnipropetrovsk region, the number of churches decreased more than fivefold (from 156 to 25), while the number of baptisms increased from 15 891 to 18 144, and church revenues increased from 586 000 to 600 000 rubles." (3)

Despite the harsh persecution that Orthodox Christianity suffered during the Soviet era, its spiritual strength, as in previous centuries, was supported by many devotees. **Doctor Luke (Voyno-Yasenetsky)** (1877–1961) was an outstanding surgeon, researcher, and practitioner, author of works on anesthesiology and purulent surgery.

---

[1] Chumachenko, T. A. The State and the Russian Orthodox Church in 1958–1964: A New Political War Against Religion, the Church, and Believers // Bulletin of Chelyabinsk State University. 2014.№ 19. Pp. 85, 87.

[2] Soskovets L. I. Religious Organizations and Believers in the Soviet State. Tomsk, 2008. P. 111.

[3] Chumachenko T. A. The State and the Russian Orthodox Church... P. 88.

who practiced medicine in the most remote corners of our country (Fig. 4.10). After the death of his beloved wife in 1919, when he was 42 years old, his religious feelings grew stronger, and he became a priest. Voino-Yasenetsky combined his service in the Church with medicine for practically his entire life, providing medical assistance to those in need. He was arrested several times and was exiled three times. Soviet officials repeatedly offered him the opportunity to manage medical institutions in exchange for renouncing his priesthood, which caused him considerable inconvenience.

Fig. 4.10. Luke (Voino-Yasenetsky)

Archbishop Luka (Voino-Yasenetsky) moved to relatively comfortable climatic and living conditions only in 1944, heading the Tambov diocese, and in 1946 he was transferred to Simferopol as Archbishop of Simferopol and Crimea. He continued to practice medicine until 1955. He was the only priest to receive the Stalin Prize (1946).

Archbishop Luke, who had an undeniable talent for journalism, sought to reconcile science and religion, pointing to the limited capabilities of human knowledge. After his death, according to reports from the Orthodox Church, people praying at the grave of the archbishop-doctor at the Holy Trinity Convent in Simferopol received **healings (1), which** prompted the Council of Bishops in 2000 to glorify him as a saint.

Matrona of Moscow (1881–1952) became even more widely known for her healing powers. The saint was born blind into a peasant family in the Tula province. From the age of 8, she became known for her ability to heal and predict the future. Thanks to the daughter of a local landowner, Matrona was able to travel with her at a young age and visited many holy places in Russia.

---

[1] Marushchak V. The Holy Surgeon. The Life of Archbishop Voin-Yasenetsky. Moscow, 2010. pp. 102–105.

Fig. 4.11. Pokrovsky Monastery (Moscow) view from Abelmanovskaya Street

Fig. 4.12. Pokrovsky Stavropegial Convent

She also met John of Kronstadt in 1899, who publicly called her "his replacement" after the end of his service. After the 1917 revolution, Matrona and her friend lived with various acquaintances. She received up to 40 people a day, practiced healing, and gave advice. Shortly before her death, when asked what those who needed her help should do after she passed away, she replied: "Come to my grave, I will always be there, I will also help you and pray for you, as I did during my lifetime" (1).

In 1998, with the blessing of Patriarch Alexy II, Matrona's relics were brought to the Danilov Monastery in Moscow and then transferred to the Pokrovsky Church on the grounds of **the Pokrovsky Monastery**. Up to 3,000 pilgrims visit the monastery every day, and on Sundays and holidays, their number reaches 25,000 (Figs. 4.11, 4.12).

The radical changes in the country's social life that began in 1917 and were accompanied by civil war and chaos also caused fundamental changes in individual consciousness, including among representatives of the old elite. **Seraphim Vyritsky** (1866–1949) — born V. N. Muravyov, a peasant's son, made a rapid career in trade, specializing in fur trading and having an annual income of up to 90 thousand rubles per year (Fig. 4.13).

Fig. 4.13. Seraphim Vyritsky

Fig. 4.14. Church of the Kazan Icon of the Mother of God in the village of Vyritsa

---

[1] Zhdanova Z. V. The Legend of the Life of the Blessed Elder Matrona. Kolomna: Holy Trinity Novo-Golutvin Monastery, 1993. P. 26.

However, in the first years of Soviet power, in new life circumstances, having refused to emigrate, he became a novice at the Alexander Nevsky Lavra. He donated all his property (including 40,000 rubles in gold coins) to the monastery.

He moved to the village of Vyritsa near St. Petersburg, once a well-known summer resort, in 1933 and remained there until his death, praying in the garden on a stone in front of an icon of Seraphim of Sarov attached to an apple tree. He is known for his prophecies and his insightful religious treatise "It Was From Me," in which he persistently and consistently develops the idea that the life and fate of an individual are determined by the activities of the Creator (Fig. 4.14).

**

The collapse of the USSR in 1991 was caused by a complex combination of internal and external factors of an objective and subjective nature (1). In spiritual terms, it was preceded, in particular, by **a formal, slogan-based commitment to the Soviet socialist state,** which did not evoke sincere emotions among citizens (Diagram 4.2). During Gorbachev's perestroika, **traditional ideological foundations** were **eroded, primarily Soviet patriotism,** through the denigration of the history of the USSR under the pretext of criticizing Stalinism.

As the country's chief ideologist, A. N. Yakovlev, admitted, it was necessary to "use Lenin's authority to strike at Stalin... And then, if successful, use Plekhanov and social democracy to strike at Lenin, liberalism and 'moral socialism' — at revolutionism in general" (2).

But it was not only cinema, general political and art magazines that deliberately and not without malice focused attention on the negative phenomena of the Soviet past. In the course of the deployment of the notorious cooperative movement, economic, domestic, and social collectivism began to erode. Overall, **the ideological, everyday, and political influence of Western individualism** is growing. **National separatism is rearing its head.**

In a hidden form, it can be traced back to the late 1950s, primarily in the Baltic states and Western Ukraine, which had recently been annexed by the USSR and were still suffering at the turn of the 1940s and 1950s.

---

[1] Gulyakov, A. D. Federalism: Mechanism of Emergence and Main Directions of Development: A Historical and Political Science Study. Moscow, 2019. P. 311.

[2] Spitsyn, E. Yu. Russia-Soviet Union. 1946–1991. Book 4. Moscow, 2021. P. 401.

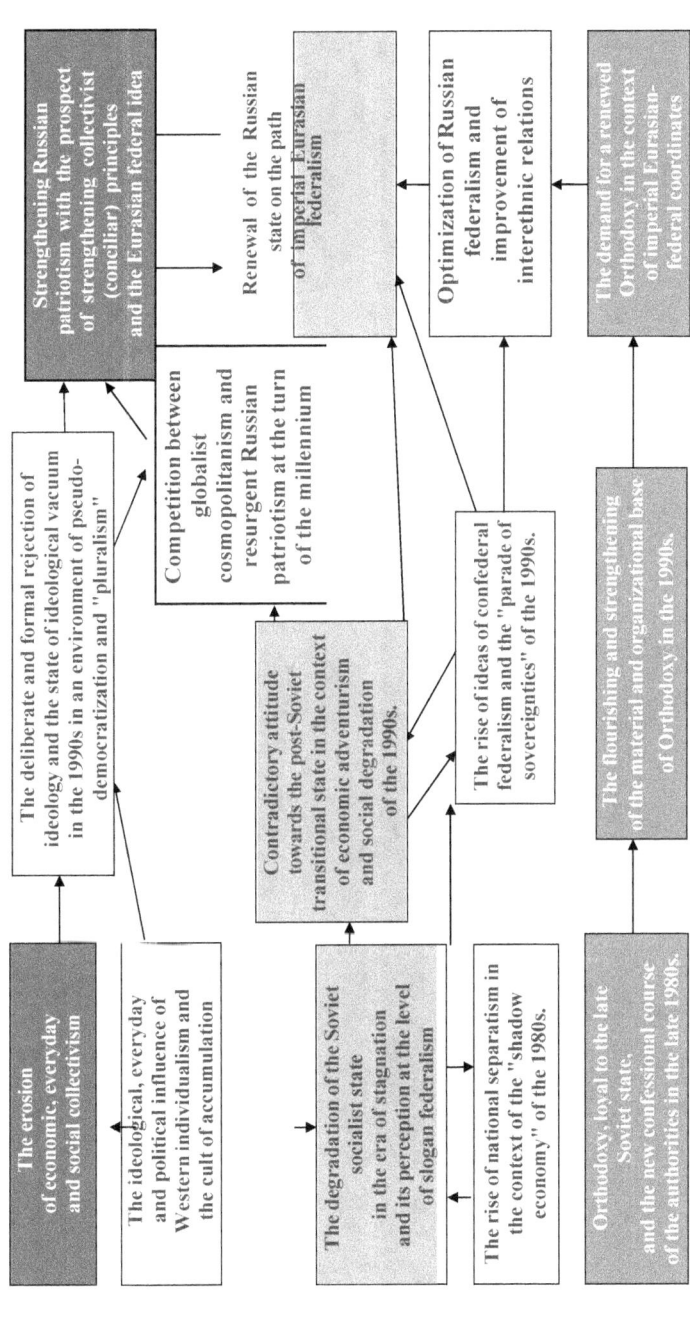

Diagram 4.2. The erosion of the spiritual core of late Soviet society and the reformatting of post-Soviet society on the basis of imperial Eurasian federalism

from the criminal underground. However, as the "shadow economy" grew in the 1970s, the illegal enrichment of certain members of society within the socialist paradigm and the desire to legitimize illegally acquired funds and achieve an increase in one's power status — primarily at the expense of the federal center — became a favorable social environment for national separatism. the desire to legitimize illegally acquired funds, and to achieve an increase in their power status — primarily at the expense of the federal center. Inadequately inflated ethnocratic claims are put forward, and ethnic tensions intensify.

In the complex situation of Gorbachev's perestroika, the Church continues to demonstrate loyalty to the Soviet state, which in turn makes deliberately conciliatory gestures towards Orthodoxy. These new relations developed under **Patriarch Pimen (S. M. Izvekov)** (1910–1990), a man with a complicated life story who had been in the camps, fought in the Great Patriotic War, and tried his hand at both secular and spiritual professions (Fig. 4.15).

Under Pimen, in 1983, the Russian Orthodox Church was given a complex of buildings of **the** former **Danilov Monastery** to establish a spiritual and administrative center (Figs. 4.16, 4.17, 4.18).

Fig. 4.15. Patriarch Pimen

Fig. 4.16. Danilov Monastery. Fortress wall

Fig. 4.17. The Patriarch's Residence

Fig. 4.18. Department of External Relations of the Moscow Patriarchate

In 1988, the 100th anniversary of the baptism of Rus was celebrated: for the first time, secular authorities took part in a purely religious event. In connection with the anniversary, a group of church hierarchs was awarded state honors. I. T. Frolov, editor-in-chief of the magazine Kommunist, put forward an initiative to publish the works of Russian religious philosophers. The pages of Moskovskie Novosti featured a landmark publication in the form of a dialogue between the prominent Soviet **historian and archaeologist V. L. Yanin and the Orthodox theologian Ioann Belevtsev.** (1) In November 1988, the Academy of Social Sciences held a round table discussion on "Problems of Freedom of Conscience in the Context of the Democratization of Soviet Society."

However, although "in 1988–1989, a record number of permits for the registration of religious societies were issued compared to previous years of 'perestroika,' the zigzags in state-confessional **policy continued."** (2)

The attitude of M. S. Gorbachev and his entourage towards the Russian Orthodox Church was not altruistic: on the one hand, party functionaries and reformers sought the support of believers, and on the other hand, they sought to destroy the established standards of socialist ideology. In turn, party workers of a traditional orientation resisted innovations that they considered unjustified.

---

[1] Spitsyn, E. Yu. Russia — Soviet Union. 1946–1991 pp. 399–400.

[2] Melnichenko, O. V. The State and the Russian Orthodox Church in Russia. 1985–1990: The Evolution of Relations // News of the Penza State Pedagogical University named after V. G. Belinsky. Humanities. 2012. No. 27. Pp. 829, 830.

***

The harsh realities of the tragic 1990s after the collapse of the USSR meant, first and foremost, a sharp weakening of the Russian state — economically, socially, and spiritually. The economic adventurism and incompetence of a narrow circle of "pseudo-reformers" led by E. Gaidar and A. Chubais, who served the interests of the West, **led to the privatization of the national economy, which was a complete failure.** In turn, cruel and ineffective experiments caused **widespread social degradation,** including that of the notorious "middle class." The models of Western liberalism, transferred to Russian soil with its traditionalist consciousness and state of deep universal social discontent, were rejected. In essence, a situational ideological vacuum formed in the mass consciousness.

Moreover, this vacuum was encouraged by the authorities as a way of dismantling the remnants of Marxist-Leninist ideology. "Obsessed with the idea of rapid entry into the Western world, the authors of the Russian Constitution, by including in it a ban on the establishment of a mandatory and state ideology... effectively allowed the values of liberal ideology to be incorporated into the structure of the Constitution as mandatory, ignoring other ideological guidelines" (1).

Moreover, **the version of liberalism imposed on society had little in common with either classical 19th-century liberalism or mid-20th-century neoliberalism.** As is well known, the core of classical liberalism was the idea of the state as a night watchman with minimal regulatory functions, which suited the self-confidently enriching industrial bourgeoisie at the time. Russian liberals at the end of the 20th century also dreamed of maximum state deregulation, but were nevertheless forced to accept certain social obligations of the state. At the same time, 19th-century liberals could not even imagine a "maximalist set of freedoms," including ultra-fashionable feminism and the promotion of sexual minorities, with which Russian liberals were forced to sympathize under pressure from the West. From Neoliberalism of the mid-20th century.

---

[1]Radikov, I. V. Searching for ideological bearings in post-Soviet Russia // MGOU Bulletin. Social Sciences. 2019.№ 1. P. 56.

Contemporary Westerners and Russian liberals also went quite far: they no longer preached the paternalistic ideal of a "welfare state" that cares for the unemployed, pensioners, and other socially disadvantaged groups. In the West in the 1990s, the concept of the "third way" became popular as a kind of compromise between state regulation and deregulation, Keynesianism and monetarism (1). However, for developing countries (including Russia), it was proposed to use the outdated recipes of classical liberalism and the slogan "the market will fix everything," which was vulgar in its senselessness.

The credo of Russian liberals in the 1990s can be defined as a deteriorated, servile version of Western globalist (globalization) neoliberalism.

Their activities as the ruling class were particularly unattractive to citizens due to their antisocial agenda.

It is characteristic that sociological studies recorded the following set of achievements and losses for the 1990s, with losses undoubtedly prevailing in the public consciousness (Table 1). The spread **of ideas of "confederative federalism"** in the 1990s had a serious destabilizing effect on public consciousness. The "parade of sovereignties" threatened to create openly separatist entities such as the Siberian, Ural, Don, and Kuban republics (2) and was accompanied by clear constitutional and legal chaos.

At that time, "some regions included provisions in their constitutions on the right to secede from Russia (Tyva); others decreed that they were states only associated with the Russian Federation (Tatarstan); , while others proclaimed that all natural resources within the territory of the republic were their property (the Republic of Sakha (Yakutia), the Republic of Altai); still others secured special conditions in agreements on the division of powers and responsibilities..." (3).

---

[1] Giddens A. Runaway World. How Globalization is Reshaping Lives. London, 2000. 140 p.

[2] Alyabieva T. K. Russia from Semi-Disintegration to Centralization // Bulletin of Moscow State Regional University. Series: History and Political Science. 2018. No. 5. P. 288.

[3] Andrichenko L. V., Yurtaeva E. A. Constitutional Foundations of Russian Federalism // Journal of Russian Law. 2013.№ 6. P. 5.

Table 1. Major achievements and losses of the 1990s in the assessment of public consciousness[1]

Achievements	Losses
1. Closure of enterprises unable to withstand competition (60%)	1. Human casualties in wars and armed conflicts (68%)
2. The opportunity to earn money without restrictions (36%)	2. The collapse of leading industries (68%)
3. The opportunity to start your own business (34%)	3. Abandonment of the idea of socialism (67%)
4. End of religious persecution (34%)	4. Decline in living standards (65%)

At the same time, the only bright spot in the spiritual atmosphere of the 1990s was **the flourishing of Orthodoxy and the strengthening of its material and organizational base.** The beginning of a new era in the life of society, the state, and the Church coincided with the election **of Patriarch Alexy II** (1929–2008) after the death of Patriarch Pimen in 1990. A descendant of a Courland noble family and the son of a protopresbyter from Tallinn, a graduate of the Leningrad Theological Academy, he was ordained bishop of Tallinn and Estonia in 1961. He was actively involved in ecumenical activities as a member of the Central Committee of the World Council of Churches and a collaborator with the apparatus and leadership of the Conference of European Churches. In 1986, he was appointed Metropolitan of Leningrad and Novgorod, and in 1990, he received the majority of votes in the election of the patriarch at the Bishops' and Local Council.

A decade after Alexy II took office "the Moscow Patriarchate included 130 dioceses, 545 monasteries (265 male and 380 female), 150 monastery podvoryes, and 19 417 parishes, where 164 bishops, 17 500 priests, and 2 300 deacons served; 5 theological academies, the St. Tikhon Theological Institute, 2 Orthodox universities, 29 seminaries, 400 theological schools, 3 diocesan women's schools, and 9 pastoral courses (a total of more than 12,000 students) Special mention should be made of the opening of the Kiev-Pechersk Lavra, the Alexander Nevsky Lavra, the Moscow Novospassky and Donskoy monasteries, the Solovetsky and Valaam monasteries, the Optina Hermitage, and the construction of the Cathedral of Christ the Savior in Moscow as centers of spiritual life. There was a The Publishing Council of

---

[1] Gorshkov, M. K. The Realities of a Transformed Russia: A Quarter Century of Social Transformations in Sociological Terms // Russia Reforming. 2018. No. 16. P. 11.

[2] Shkarovsky, M. V. The Russian Orthodox Church in the 20th... p. 422.

Fig. 4.19. Metropolitan Ioann (Snychev) of Leningrad (1927–1995)

the Moscow Patriarchate was established, publishing houses appeared at monasteries and churches, and more than 200 Orthodox mass periodicals began to be published[1].

The 1990s are also remembered for the activities of such an outstanding hierarch of the Orthodox Church as **Metropolitan John** (Snychev) **of Leningrad** (1927–1995) (Fig. 4.19).

He was awarded a doctorate in church history for a series of works and a course of lectures on the history of the Russian Orthodox Church in the 1920s. He was sharply criticized by Russian liberals for his monarchism, nationalism, and anti-Westernism.

He published articles in the patriotic newspapers Sovetskaya Rossiya and Zavtra. He denounced democracy for allowing the "principle of quantitative superiority" to open the door to "unrestrained abuse." In his opinion, only authoritative representatives of their classes, estates, and ethnic groups could be "responsible electors."

***

With the loss of their monopoly on power in the early 2000s, Russian liberals have seen a reformatting of ideological preferences. "According to sociological studies, the value of freedom was central to Russians in the 1990s. But by the early 2000s, citizens had become 'tired' of freedom (and even more so of permissiveness), and the values of security and stability came to the fore... With the onset of the global economic crisis in 2008... patriotism, statehood, and identity became the most relevant values " (2). In particular, VTsIOM 2011 demonstrates a strengthening of sentiments in favor of state regulation and a sharp decline in interest in economic liberalization (Table 2).

---

[1] Shkarovsky, M. V. The Russian Orthodox Church in the 20th Century... p. 420.

[2] Vasilenko, I. A. Dynamics of Political Values in the Process of Mobilization of Modern Russia // News of Tula State University. Humanities. 2016.№ 4. P. 63–67.

Table 2. **Citizens' preferences in the field of economic policy**[1]

Proposed options for change in the country	Respondents' answers (in %)
Strengthening the role of the state in all spheres of life, nationalization of large enterprises and industries, strict suppression of corruption, restriction of capital outflow	62
Liberalization of all spheres of life, freeing business from the power of officials, increasing competition, unleashing citizens' initiative	18
Let everything remain as it is	12
Other option	1
I find it difficult to answer	8

Against the backdrop of worsening relations with the West and increasing international turbulence, there is a struggle between two ideological poles — Westernization and anti-Westernization (nativism). The old ideological dispute of the 19th and early 20th centuries is being revived in the new historical conditions of rapidly advancing globalization.

Westernizers level accusations at their opponents:
"1) Compared to Europe, Russia is a backward country, and therefore insisting on this backwardness leads to destructiveness in following a "populist policy"; 2) The ideas are vague and undeveloped, that is, there is no clear program of necessary social changes..." (2) In turn, **the non-Westernizers** put forward counterarguments: "One may doubt that the Westernizers wish Russia and the Russian people well... It can be said that Westerners hinder global development by transferring the private experience of Europe to other cultures and countries... Finally, it is also possible to take the position that the current development of Europe is misguided and leading to disaster..."(3).

Economists, geopoliticians, sociologists, political scientists, and historians have been hotly debating Russia's place in the modern world and the best ideology for it for the past two decades. Doctor of Economics, Head of the Center for Post-Industrial Society Studies **V. L. Inozemtsev** in his numerous monographs and articles (including Beyond the Economic Society:

---

[1] VTsIOM: press release№ 1931. Prospects for the right wing in Russia. URL: wciom.ru/index.php? id=459&uid=112352 (accessed: 12.11.2012).

[2] Blekher L. I., Lyubarsky G. Yu. The main Russian debate: from Westernizers and Slavophiles to globalism and the New Middle Ages. Moscow, 2003. P. 97.

[3] Ibid. p. 105.

Post-Industrial Theories and Post-Economic Trends in the Modern World. Moscow, 1998; The Limits of Catching Up. Moscow, 2000; "The Lost Decade," Moscow, 2013), he critically assesses Russia's socio-economic course in the context of globalization. He justifies globalization itself very gently and unobtrusively, condemning anti-globalists and supporters of "limited globalization" for their lack of effective proposals (1), while sharply criticizing foreign policy for its "imperialism." (2)

Academician **T. I. Zaslavskaya** (1927–2013) — founder of Russian economic sociology, director-organizer of the All-Union Center for the Study of Public Opinion, researched the social mechanisms of the transforming post-communist economy. In the early 2000s, she was quite critical of the transformations in Russia, although she did not reject the Western vector of development. In her opinion,

"**The Soviet** institutional system has been irreversibly destroyed, and Russia's current basic instruments are transitional in nature and are unlikely to be much more effective than their Soviet counterparts. The formation of a coherent system of liberal democratic institutions, which form the basis of the rule of law, is still in its early **stages**." (3) Sociologist, candidate of political sciences, director of the Institute for Globalization and Social Movements, author of the book "Peripheral Empire: Cycles of Russian History" (Moscow, 2009) and From Empires to Imperialism (Moscow, 2010), combines left-wing anti-globalization beliefs with a commitment to the ideas of Western social democracy. In his opinion, although "Soviet civilization" was an "unconditional reality" that developed for some time in conditions of economic self-isolation, "there is not and cannot be a 'Russian civilization' due to Russia's integration into the global economy in conditions of as local

---

[1] Inozemtsev V. L. Contemporary Globalization and Its Perception in the World // Universal and Global History (The Evolution of the Universe, Earth, Life, and Society). Reader. Volgograd, 2012. Pp. 493–507.

[2] Inozemtsev V. L. On intersecting post-imperial "peripheries" // Untouchable Reserve. 2021. № 1. Pp. 3–14.

[3] Zaslavskaya, T. I. Contemporary Russian Society: Problems and Prospects // Social Sciences and Modernity. 2004. № 5. P. 14.

markets and economies merge into a single capitalist world market..." (1).

Historian, orientalist, and religious scholar **A. B. Zubov**, PhD in History, served as editor-in-chief of the Russian-international book project "History of Russia in the 20th Century," which provoked a mixed reaction due to its highly critical attitude toward Russian history.

Zubov himself interprets Russia as an "incorrectly developed" country. According to his angry rhetorical assessment, "properly developing nations do not leave behind them ditches filled with millions of compatriots killed by their own terrorist regime, do not destroy their cultural and spiritual values with satanic obsession, do not plunder their native land to the ground, exporting the treasures they have extracted overseas and condemning most of their fellow citizens to poverty and lawlessness, nor do they tolerate statues of bloody murderers and treacherous corrupters in the squares of their cities. But we have all of this in abundance. Our people are seriously ill."

Fig. 4.20. M. G. Delyagin

On the other side of the political barricades were also representatives of various humanities. Dr. economic sciences, research director of the Institute for Problems globalization, State Duma deputy **M. G. Delyagin** contributed to the critical study of the globalizing world (in particular, he developed a theory of the formation of a global ruling class).

Fig. 4.21. S. Yu. Glazyev

He is the author of the books "Russia for Russians" (Moscow, 2007), "Russia's Revenge" (Moscow, 2008), "Russia in the Face of History. The End of an Era of National Betrayal?" (Moscow, 2015), two-volume work "The End of an Era. Caution: Doors Opening. Vol. 1. General Theory of Globalization. Vol. 2. Special History of Globalization" (Moscow, 2019, 2020) (Fig. 4.20).

---

[1] Kagarlitsky, B. Yu. From Empires to Imperialism: The State and the Emergence of Bourgeois Civilization. Moscow, 2010. P. 30.

[2] Zubov, A. B. Russia: Continuation of History? // Politia. 2011.№ 3. pp. 22, 23.

Academician S. Yu. Glazyev, who served as Advisor to the President of the Russian Federation from 2012 to 2019, is the author of the concept of technological structures (large complexes of technologically related industries) with a life cycle of about a century and a period of dominance of about 40 years. According to **S. Yu. Glazyev**, the new, sixth technological structure began around 2010, and its period of widespread use will fall between 2018 and 2040. It is important that Russia, having rejected Western monetarist recipes, has entered a new long wave of economic growth with its own strategy of advanced development (1) (Fig. 4.21).

Lithologist and Doctor of Philosophy **A. S. Panarin** (1940–2003), a critic of globalism and consumer society, also advocated for Russia's own original path of development. His works Russia in the Civilizational Process between Atlanticism and Eurasianism (Moscow, 1995), Russia in the Cycles of World History (Moscow, 1999), Global Political Forecasting (Moscow, 2001), and Orthodox Civilization in the Global World (Moscow, 2002) condemn the integration of our country into a foreign policy based on social Darwinism and apologetic globalism.

A similar position was also held by geopolitician, Doctor of Political Science and Doctor of Sociology **A. G. Dugin**, leader of the International Eurasian Movement, which has branches in 29 countries[2]. A. G. Dugin is considered a theorist of neo-Eurasianism, combining Russian traditions and the modernist avant-garde. This is evidenced by his works such as "The Foundations of Eurasianism" (Moscow, 2002), "The Geopolitics of Postmodernism" (Moscow, 2007), Geopolitics of Russia (Moscow, 2012), and Russia's Eurasian Revenge (Moscow, 2014).

Anti-Western sentiments are quite common among historians. In particular, the activities of the long-time dean of the history department at St. Petersburg University, Doctor of Historical Sciences **I. Ya. Froyanov** (1936–2020), caused a great public resonance. His original theory about the pre-class communal nature and veche power of Novgorod Rus raises questions among experts (1). His assessment of the October Revolution and the collapse of the USSR (2) has its supporters and opponents, as does his harsh criticism of Boris Yeltsin's regime (3).

---

[1] Glazyev, S. Yu. Strategy for Russia's Advanced Development in the Context of the Global Crisis. Moscow, 2010. pp. 55–69, 78–80, 220–225, 238–249.

[2] International Eurasian Movement. URL: http://google.com/search?q=International+Eurasian+Movement&oq (accessed: 24.08.2022).

Professors of the History Department of Lomonosov Moscow State University, Doctors of Historical Sciences **A. I. Vdovin and A. S. Barsenkov** (4) also contributed to the critical analysis of the 1990s.

A. I. Vdovin is known as an expert on issues of Soviet federalism and ethnic history (5). A. S. Barsenkov specializes in the history of our country in the 1980s and 1990s. (6). A. I. Vdovin expressed his view of contemporary history as follows: "After the collapse of the USSR and the world socialist system, the end of history did not come. Socialism has not ceased to exist; it is developing in Chinese and Kuban variants." At the same time, "it is impossible to modernize all of humanity according to the American model due to the limited nature of Earth's resources..." In Russia, changes have recently been visible in public consciousness and politics: "While in the 1990s the media actively called on Russians to condemn their imperial past and aspirations for great power, not to cling to 'archaic national ideals,' to realize the 'rosy dream of Russian cosmopolitanism,' and to finally become part of Europe, then recently the official rhetoric has been changing..." and previously forbidden words "nation" and "empire" gained recognition (7).

The renewal of the structures of the Russian state, which has been particularly noticeable against the backdrop of increasing international turbulence since the beginning of 2010, has been accompanied by a strengthening of patriotism and the Eurasian imperial federalist idea. Moreover In structural terms, the understanding of patriotism is clearly complicated: it may "include (in varying proportions) the following ideologemes:

---

[1] Froyanov, I. Ya. Kievan Rus'. Essays on Social and Political History. L., 1980 ; Ancient Rus'. An Attempt to Study the History of Social and Political Struggle. M. ; SPb. : Zlatoust, 1995.

[2] Froyanov, I. Y. October Seventeen (Looking from the Present). St. Petersburg, 1997.

[3] Froyanov, I. Ya. Plunge into the Abyss (Russia at the End of the 20th Century). 2nd ed. St. Petersburg, 2001.

[4] Barsenkov, A. S., Vdovin, A. I. History of Russia: 1917–2004: Textbook for university students. Moscow, 2005.

[5] Vdovin, A. I. Russians in the 20th Century. Moscow, 2013.

[6] Barsenkov, A. S. Gorbachev's Reforms and the Fate of the Union State (1985–1991). Moscow, 2001; Barsenkov, A. S. Introduction to Modern Russian History (1985–1991). Moscow, 2002.

[7] Vdovin, A. I. USSR: History of a Great Power. 1922–1991. Moscow, 2019. pp. 4, 5, 10.

– sovereign democracy;
– controlled democracy and political stability;
– innovative economic development;
– the revival of a great power of global significance" (1).

One can partly agree with this perception of the phenomenon of patriotism. "Patriotism, apparently, should be understood as a stable attitude and conscious love for one's family, nation, national and cultural identity, the Fatherland in its past and present, a willingness to serve it, to defend and protect its goals, ideals, and values of other peoples, their families, and citizens (i.e., to be tolerant as well)" (2). However, with regard to the last characteristic, related to respect for other peoples, it should be clarified that this obviously does not refer to all ethnic groups around the world, but only to those living within a particular state. Patriotism is always as specific as possible and, in its common usage, does not imply internationalism or globalism.

However, the most important thing for Russians is that it is associated with the legacy of Eurasian ideology and federal civil culture. **Eurasianists**, who were in exile in the 1920s and 1930s, contributed greatly to the formation of modern anti-Western, geopolitical, and state-legal thought. Their predecessors in Muscovy can be considered the elders Philotheus and Nil Sorsky, and in the first half of the 19th century, M. L. Magnitsky (1778–1855) and the Slavophiles, and later N. Ya. Danilevsky and K. N. Leontiev. At the same time, the Eurasianists completely rejected the Pan-Slavic idea, pointing out that the Eastern Slavs had been strongly influenced by **the Turanian ethno-psychological type** (i.e., the Ugric-Finnish, Turkic, Mongolian, Manchu, and Samoyed peoples). This ethnic group "is distinguished by clarity and systematicity of thinking, as well as peace of mind based on a strong subconscious conviction in the correctness of the chosen worldview. The system of ideas about the surrounding reality, if only it satisfies requirements

---

[1] Shatilov A. B. Formation of the concept of state patriotism in Russia in the period 2000–2017: main stages and basic ideologemes // Humanities. Bulletin of the Financial University. 2017.№ 3. P. 23.

[2] Tusko V. S. Some aspects of the formation of national ideology in Russia // Cossacks. 2015. No. 10. P. 15.

of accessibility and logical consistency, accepted by the entire nation without causing any controversy afterwards. If a worldview is borrowed from another people, it does not undergo serious changes" (1). It was precisely these socio-psychological characteristics of the Turans, which influenced the Slavs — especially during the time of the Golden Horde — that allowed the Slavs to become the unifiers of Eurasia.

One of the founders of Eurasianism, geographer and economist **P. N. Savitsky** (1895–1968), believed that Russian culture belonged neither to Europe nor to Asia. "Eurasian culture is connected with other cultures, but Asian culture is closer to it." Linguist and cultural scholar **N. S. Trubetskoy** (1880–1938) took a more rigid anti-Western stance. Russia should not be a "province of European civilization"; it is necessary to "create an independent and self-governing Russian-Eurasian **culture**" (3). "The Romano-Germanic world," notes N. S. Trubetskoy," is **our worst enemy; we must ruthlessly crush and trample the idols of Western social ideals.** "The distinguished historian **G. V. Vernadsky** (1887–1973) noted that Russia, occupying the space of "great lowlands — the plains of the White Sea-Caucasus, Western Siberia, and Turkestan" (5), ensured its long-term existence. Its key advantage was its intermediate position, essentially mediating between the forest and the steppe, and the organization of the state in the form of a military empire. The jurist **N. N. Alekseev** (1879–1964), with the aim of defining the national idea of the state, studied the views of the Cossacks, schismatics, and sectarians and came to the conclusion that the national political ideal could be found in a combination of Orthodox monarchy, dictatorship, Cossack freedom, and a sectarian understanding of the state. Although hostile to Bolshevism, N. N. Alekseev recognized its strength, noting: "The Bolsheviks, who carried out Pugachev's cause in 1917 , "Theft" was transformed into the communist system, and the Soviet regime replaced the Cossack tsar. The strength of this regime "was revealed mainly in the fact that it replaced direct Cossack

---

[1] Romanovskaya V. B., Krymov A. V. The Eurasian Doctrine of State and Law. N. Novgorod, 2010. P. 14.

[2] Russia and Europe. Reader on Russian Geopolitics. Moscow, 2007. pp. 410–411.

[3] Trubetskoy N. S. The Legacy of Genghis Khan. Moscow, 1999. pp. 282–285.

[4] History of Political and Legal Doctrines: Textbook for Universities / Edited by Prof. O. V. Martyshin. Moscow, 2002. P. 849.

[5] Vernadsky G. V. An Outline of Russian History. Moscow, 2004. P. 24.

Fig. 4.22. The founders of Eurasianism

democracy was replaced by a uniquely structured people's state based on a combination of dictatorship and popular representation (1) (Fig. 4.22).

The ideal for N. N. Alekseev and the Eurasianists was **a Eurasian federation** — a state that would reject the Bolshevik slogan of national self-determination and be based on the principle of economic and geographical characteristics in the organization of its constituent entities. At the same time, N. N. Alekseev was opposed to a single template for reformatting the Soviet federation in the future, after the Bolsheviks left power. He also valued the flexible experience of Soviet federalism. "Based on the fact that Given that the

---

[1] Alekseev, N. N. The Russian People and the State. Moscow, 1998. P. 115.

Soviet Union demonstrates various types of relationships between the parts and the whole, as well as a great diversity of its constituent parts, it is possible to speak of the existence of a wide range of options and types of federation within it. This circumstance, Alekseev believed, allows various states to join the Soviet Union as independent members on a very diverse and free basis, provided that they accept the Soviet state system. (1)

In post-Soviet Russia, as its influence is restored, the ideals **of neo-Eurasianism** and its most prominent representative, **A. G. Dugin**, are gaining ground. Although he is accused of having "lost all the mesmerizing originality of the philosophical worldview of classical Eurasianism in his political aspirations" (2), in fact, the desire to politicize public thought in the era of globalization should only be welcomed. As the leader of the international Eurasian movement, he states that at present "the influence of Eurasianism is very multidimensional and multifaceted, encompassing both the expert community and the scientific academic community, politicians and the military, as well as economists" (3). At the same time, other variants of modern Eurasianism, such as Kazakh or Turkish (especially if they exploit the ideas of Pan-Turkism), may not always be successful or useful. After all, "the ideology of Eurasianism was created, supported, and developed by Russians," although "there is room for everyone in Eurasianism — for Kalmyks (Mongols), Jews, and Georgians" (4).

Throughout history, various formats of a unified civilization have emerged — the empire of Genghis Khan, the Russian Empire, the Soviet Union... "In this regard, all forms that unite Eurasia have a certain common style — a special territory that is not integrated into either Europe or China.

---

[1] Kovalenko V. I., Fedyakin A. V. Problems of federalism in the works of Russian émigré thinkers // Bulletin of Moscow University. Series 12. Political Sciences. 2011. No. 6. P. 62.

[2] Isaeva, O. S. Modification of the philosophical ideas of classical Eurasianism in the creative legacy of A. G. Dugin // Philosophical Thought. 2019. № 7. P. 9.

[3] Eurasianism as a non-Western episteme of Russian humanities. Interview with Alexander Gelievich Dugin, Doctor of Political Science, Doctor of Sociology, Professor, leader of the International Eurasian Movement // RUDN Bulletin. International Relations Series. 2022. Vol. 22, № 1. P. 145.

[4] Ibid. p. 146.

Iranian, Indian, or Semitic civilizations" (1). Eurasianism is currently attracting interest in many parts of the world: in China, Iran. "In Pakistan and even in the Arab world, which has practically no connection to Eurasia, interest in Eurasianism is awakening. Even in Europe, interest is emerging: some representatives **of patriotic circles say that Europe should join Eurasia and move away from America.**" (2)

A modern **imperial federal ideology** should be formed on the basis of Eurasianism. The USSR was quite rightly perceived as an empire, and the Russian Federation continues its traditions. There is no reason to assert, as V. Solovey does, "that Russians have ceased to be an imperial people." In fact, "imperial thinking is closely linked to our mentality..." (3). Our modern empire can grow through confederative additions along its borders, which over time have the potential to become federalized (e.g., South Ossetia, Abkhazia, Donetsk and Luhansk Republics).

The main thing is that this federal empire is permeated by a growing **spirit of unity** (Russian and Eurasian collectivism). Incidentally, this spirit of unity is embedded in such an important integrative, authoritative, and consultative body as **the State Council,** which serves as a platform for communication between the legislative and executive branches of government and federal and regional officials.

Russian federalism must be improved in specific areas without changing its highly centralized nature, whether it concerns the economic specialization of regions and financial assistance to local businesses, the autonomy of constituent entities in lawmaking, the promotion of a federal civic culture, or the enhancement of the authority of the Federation Council (4).

---

[1] Eurasianism as a non-Western episteme of Russian humanities. Interview with Alexander Gelievich Dugin, Doctor of Political Science, Doctor of Sociology, Professor, leader of the International Eurasian Movement // RUDN Bulletin. International Relations Series. 2022. Vol. 22, № 1. P. 147.

[2] Ibid. p. 147.

[3] Marchukov, A. N. Prospects for the Development of Modern Russia: The Imperial Path or the Nation State // Bulletin of Volgograd State University. Series 4. History. Regional Studies. International Relations. 2008. No. 2. Pp. 113, 114.

[4] Gulyakov, A. D. Concept of State and Legal Policy in the Sphere of Federal Relations (draft). Penza, 2020.

Along with the revival of a strong Russian state and statist ideology, the renewal of Orthodox Christianity on strictly patriotic and imperial-federalist positions is of great importance, as can be seen under **Patriarch Kirill** (born V. M. Gundyaev). The son of the chief mechanic of the Kalinin factory and later an Orthodox priest, he graduated from the Leningrad Theological Seminary and the Leningrad Theological Academy, and in 1974 he became the head of these educational institutions (Fig. 4.23).

While holding a spiritual rank, he was actively involved in external church relations, which allowed him to actively defend the interests of the Russian Orthodox Church after becoming patriarch in 2009.

Church on the international stage. It was he, as Metropolitan of Smolensk and Kaliningrad, who in 1993 became the main organizer of the World Russian People's Council, a progressive, patriotically oriented forum.

Fig. 4.23. Patriarch Kirill

"The ideological basis for the leading role of the Church was the concepts of 'Russian civilization', 'East Slavic civilization', and 'Russian world', the main author of which was Metropolitan Kirill of Kaliningrad and Smolensk (since 2009 — Patriarch Kirill)" (1). In 2007, largely thanks to him, an act was signed on canonical communion between the Russian Orthodox Church Abroad and the Russian Orthodox Church of the Moscow Patriarchate. The Orthodox Church's relations with the Russian Foreign Ministry became more systematic: religious buildings began to be built at embassies, and Orthodox literature began to be distributed.

In 2016, Russian Orthodoxy took a patriotic, anti-globalist position towards the Patriarchate of Constantinople (Ecumenical Patriarchate) and refused to participate in the Pan-Orthodox Council. Against this backdrop, the following appear more promising were contacts with Pope Francis in Havana — they were conducted on the basis of equality between the parties and social constructivism.

---

[1] Lunkin R. N. The Church and Foreign Policy: From the "Russian World" to Globalization // Via in tempore. History. Political Science. 2018.№ 1.

Meanwhile, **Patriarch Bartholomew of Constantinople**, pursuing his ideological and religious expansion, intervened in a purely political conflict between three Orthodox churches, which was initiated by the pro-Western Ukrainian regime: **the Ukrainian Orthodox Church of the Moscow Patriarchate (UOC-MP), the Ukrainian Orthodox Church of the Kiev Patriarchate (UOC-KP), and the Ukrainian Autocephalous Church (UAC).**

Until 2018, when the Kiev authorities began seizing religious buildings in the interests of the UOC-KP, the UOC-MP was the dominant denomination, with the exception of three regions of Galicia (Lviv, Ivano-Frankivsk, and Ternopil). It had 12,069 parishes and 251 monasteries, while the UOC-KP had only 5,114 parishes and 60 monasteries. The UAOC was the third most important religious denomination, with[1] 195 parishes and 13 monasteries (1).

The appeal of the Ukrainian Verkhovna Rada to **Patriarch Bartholomew of Constantinople in** July 2016 to grant autocephaly to the Orthodox Church in Ukraine gave the legal start to the process of confessional separation. In April 2018, President P. Poroshenko, after holding formal negotiations with representatives of the UOC-KP, the UAOC, and the UOC-MP and failing to achieve complete unity with the Moscow-oriented Orthodox clergy, nevertheless appealed to Patriarch Bartholomew to grant **a tomos of autocephaly.**

Last summer, in 2018, he proclaimed that he considered Ukraine to be his canonical responsibility and that the principle of the Moscow Patriarchate, which had exercised patronage over this territory since 1686, was unfounded. In doing so, "Bartholomew effectively usurped the right to interfere in the affairs of other churches, which had not been the case before: although the Patriarchate of Constantinople bore the title of 'Ecumenical', it was a right among equals, but by no means the right of a feudal lord over his vassals" (2). Unfortunately, the religious conflict in Ukraine continues, and with the start of the special operation on February 24, 2022, it is taking on a new dimension.

The Russian Orthodox Church, led by Patriarch Kirill, is facing intense pressure from the international community. I would like to express my confidence that, despite the externally fueled trend toward church separation, a federation of Orthodox churches led by the Moscow Patriarchate will emerge in Europe.

---

[1] Kurylev K. P., Stanis D. V. The church schism in Ukraine as a consequence of the coup d'état in February 2014 // Post-Soviet Studies. 2019. Vol. 2, No. 2. Pp. 966–967.

[2] Ibid. P. 970.

Despite the dominance of Soviet principles in public life, our country preserves its Orthodox tradition. "... based on the ethnic principle of calculating religious affiliation in Russia today: 120 million Orthodox Christians, 600 000 Catholics, more than a million believers of the Armenian Apostolic Church, 14 million Muslims, 230 000 Jews, and 90 000 Buddhists." At the same time, data on religious self-identification significantly qualifies these judgments: according to various surveys, 55–59% of Russian citizens, or up to 82% of Russian people, consider themselves Orthodox (i.e., 70–85 million people) (1). And that's quite a lot! And although, according to other data "only 5% of the population who call themselves Orthodox Christians regularly attend church" (2), the main thing is not adherence to ritual, but the conviction and sincerity of the people. At the same time, attention is drawn to "the widespread and increasingly frequent baptism of infants, the presence of young children in churches, ... the approximate equality of elderly ... and middle-aged parishioners, and the gradual increase in the number of men among them" (3).

---

[1] Filatov, S., Lunkin, R. Statistics on Russian religiosity: the magic of numbers and ambiguous reality // SOCIS. 2005. No. 6. Pp. 35–45.

[2] Leksin V. N. Russian Orthodoxy Today // Contours of Global Transformations. 2018. No. 4. P. 69.

[3] Ibid. P. 70.

CONCLUSION

Russian society and the Russian state are relatively young. For example, compared to imperial China, which has a history of more than two thousand years, and if we take into account the pre-imperial period, more than three thousand years.

At the same time, the core of Russian civilization was formed gradually. Its basis was Orthodox Christianity, brought to Kievan Rus' at the end of the 10th century by Prince Vladimir, with all other elements serving as additions to it in subsequent historical eras.

To summarize, the numerous spiritual core with temporary mobile elements formed the spiritual strength of Russian statehood, which we could represent as a triangle (diagram).

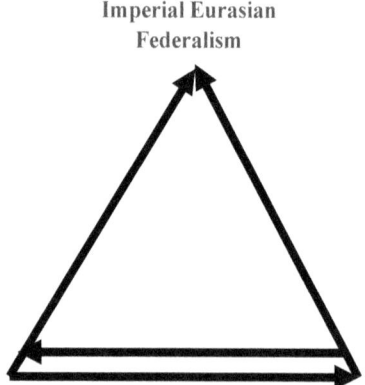

Imperial Eurasian Federalism

Commitment to the conservative (anti-Western) Orthodox tradition

Collectivism and conciliarity

The spiritual strength of Russian statehood

Orthodox conservatism in its anti-Western orientation is the most stable element of the Russian spiritual structure. Of course, one can discuss the merits and shortcomings of Westernism and nativism (anti-Westernism), noting that "Westerners are more prone to sins of reason (thoughtlessness) and atrophy of feeling (ruthlessness, indifference)," while "nativists should be more afraid of sins of feeling (national egoism, fanaticism) and atrophy of reason (lack of a well-developed position)" (1). However, Russia is too large as a geopolitical entity and too independent in socio-economic terms to be directly associated with its Western neighbors.

Moreover, the West is not friendly towards Russia.

In a short article in 1949, I. A. Ilyin noted many negative emotions among Europeans toward Russia — fear, arrogance, hostility, envy, and ignorance. "Europeans need a bad Russia: **barbaric**, so that they can 'civilise' it in their own way; **threatening in size**, so that it can be divided up; **aggressive**, so that a coalition can be organised against it; **reactionary**, so that revolution can be justified and a republic demanded; **religiously decadent,** so that they can break into it with propaganda for the Reformation or Catholicism; **economically insolvent,** so that they can claim its "unused" spaces, its raw materials, or at least lucrative trade agreements **and concessions."** (2).

Russian collectivism — initially communal, and later also conciliar—is the most important feature of spiritual life. **Most Western nations are individualistic (3), and for this reason alone, they cannot** understand Russians. "Western Christians, both Catholics and Protestants, usually find it difficult to understand what conciliarity is... Sobornost... is the opposite of both Catholic authoritarianism and Protestant individualism; it means communitarianism, which knows no external authority above itself, but also knows no individualistic seclusion and isolation... (4)

---

[1] Blecher, L. I., Lyubarsky, G. Yu. The Main Russian Debate: From Westernizers and Slavophiles to Globalism and the New Middle Ages. Moscow, 2003. P. 117.

[2] Ilyin, I. A. World Politics of Russian Sovereigns // Professor I. A. Ilyin. Our Tasks. Articles 1948–1954. Vol. 1. Paris: Published by the Russian Military Union. 1956. P. 93.

[3] Salomatin A. Yu. Modernization of the State in Europe, the USA, and Russia (Comparative Analysis of Concrete Models of Democratic Advance). Penza, 2013. pp. 114–118.

4 Berdyaev, N. A. The Russian Idea. Thinkers of the Russian Diaspora. St. Petersburg, 1992. P. 180.

It is necessary not to contrast socio-political and religious-philosophical unity, as the Slavophiles did. It is important to see unity in combination with collectivism as one of the pillars of Russian spiritual strength.

How could such a vast state and such an original people be governed? Initially occupying the space at the junction of the steppe and the forest, it managed to build up its vitality in the safer but economically poorer forest territories, absorbing the administrative experience of the great empires — Byzantium and the Golden Horde. The authoritarian, autocratic imperial style of governance developed elements of federalism, which transformed into a full-fledged and original Soviet federalism. In fact, it was created on the basis of Eurasian solidarity and imperialism and should continue to develop in the same direction. This is what gives Russian statehood its stability and most fully characterizes its spiritual strength.

LIST OF REFERENCES

Scientific and educational literature

1. Administrative-Territorial Structure of Russia. — Moscow, 2002.
2. Ayermajer, K. Politics and Culture under Lenin and Stalin. 1917–1932 / K. Ayermajer. — Moscow, 1998.
3. Aksakov, I. S. On the Truth of Russian Politics / I. S. Aksakov // Complete Works. — Moscow, 1886.
4. Aksakov, K. S. The State and the People / K. S. Aksakov. — Moscow: Institute of Russian Civilization, 2009.
5. Alekseev, S. V. The Proto-Slavs / S. V. Alekseev. — Moscow, 2015.
6. Alekseev, S. V. Slavic Europe in the 5th–8th Centuries / S. V. Alekseev. — Moscow, 2002.
7. Alekseeva, T. I. Ethnogenesis of the Eastern Slavs Based on Anthropological Data / T. I. Alekseeva. — Moscow, 1973.
8. Andreeva, I. Private Life under Socialism. The Experience of a Soviet Citizen / I. Andreeva. — Moscow, 2009.
9. Babkin, M. A. The Clergy of the Russian Orthodox Church and the Overthrow of the Monarchy (Early 20th Century – Late 1917) / M. A. Babkin. — Moscow, 2007.
10. Balalikin, D. A. Problems of the "Priesthood" and "Kingdom" in Russia in the Second Half of the 17th Century. Moscow: Vest, 2006.
11. Bezotosny, V. M. Russia and Europe in the era of 1812. Strategy and geopolitics / V. M. Bezotosny. — Moscow, 2012.
12. Belenchuk, L. N. The Enlightenment in Russia. The View of Westernizers and Slavophiles / L. N. Belenchuk. — Moscow, 2015.
13. Belyaev, I. D. The Zemsky System in Russia / I. D. Belyaev. — St. Petersburg: Nauka, 2004.
14. Beskrovny, L. G. The Patriotic War of 1812 / L. G. Beskrovny. — Moscow, 1962.
15. Blocher, L. I. The Main Russian Debate: From Westernizers and Slavophiles to Globalism and the New Middle Ages / L. I. Blocher, G. Yu. Lyubarsky. — Moscow, 2003.
16. Bondarenko, V. V. Holy Elders / V. V. Bondarenko. — Moscow: Molodaya Gvardiya, 2020.

17. Borisov, N. S. Church Figures of Medieval Rus in the 13th–18th Centuries / N. S. Borisov. — Moscow: Moscow State University Press, 1988.
18. Bokhanov, A. N. Emperor Alexander III / A. N. Bokhanov. — Moscow, 1998.
19. Bokhanov, A. N. Nicholas II / A. N. Bokhanov. — Moscow, 1998.
20. Brandenberger, D. L. National Bolshevism. Stalinist Mass Culture and the Formation of Russian National Identity (1931–1956) / D. L. Brandenberger. — Saint Petersburg, 2009.
21. Bredikhin, A. L. Political and Legal Views of Westernizers in Russia in the 19th Century: The Interconnection between Political Ideology and Understanding of Law / A. L. Bredikhin, D. A. Rudenko. — Moscow, 2016.
22. Brikker, A. The History of Peter the Great. The History of Catherine II. Complete edition in one volume / A. Brikker. — Moscow, 2017.
23. Valishchevsky, K. Peter the Great. The Kingdom of Women. The Daughter of Peter the Great. Complete edition in one volume / K. Valishchevsky. — Moscow, 2017.
24. Vasilyev, L. S. History of the East / L. S. Vasilyev. — Moscow, 1993. — Vol. 1.
25. Vasilyeva, O. Yu. The Russian Orthodox Church in the Politics of the Soviet State. 1943–1948 / O. Yu. Vasilyeva. — Moscow, 2001.
26. Vdovin, A. I. Russians in the 20th Century / A. I. Vdovin. — Moscow, 2013.
27. Vdovin, A. I. The USSR: History of a Great Power (1922–1991) / A. I. Vdovin. — Moscow, 2019.
28. Velichko, A. M. The Church and the Emperor in Byzantine and Russian History (Historical and Legal Essays) / A. M. Velichko. — Saint Petersburg, 2006.
29. Verbitskaya, O. M. Russian Peasantry: From Stalin to Khrushchev / O. M. Verbitskaya. — Moscow, 1992.
30. Vernadsky, G. The Moscow Kingdom / G. Vernadsky. — Moscow, 2017.
31. Vert, N. History of the Soviet State / N. Vert. — Moscow, 1995.
32. Viola, L. Peasant Rebellion in the Stalin Era: Collectivization and the Culture of Peasant Resistance / L. Viola. — Moscow, 2010.
33. Vodarsky, Ya. E. Orthodox Monasteries of Russia and Their Role in the Development of Culture (11th – Early 20th Centuries) / Ya. E. Vodarsky, E. G. Istomina. — Moscow, 2009.
34. Volkov, F. D. The Collapse of British Policy and Diplomatic Isolation of the Soviet State (1917–1924) / F. D. Volkov. — Moscow, 1954.
35. Vorobyova, S. A. Philosophical and Historical Ideas in Russia (1830–1850s) / S. A. Vorobyova. — Saint Petersburg, 2010.
36. Voronin, N. N. Architecture of Northeastern Russia in the 12th–15th Centuries / N. N. Voronin. — Moscow, 1961.

37. Geraskina, Yu. V. Relations between the Russian Orthodox Church, Society, and the Authorities in the Late 1930s–1991 (Based on Materials from Regions of Central Russia) / Yu. V. Geraskina. — Moscow, 2008.
38. Gimpelson, E. G. The Formation of the Soviet Political System 1917–1923 / E. G. Gimpelson. — Saint Petersburg, 2005.
39. Grabar, I. E. On Russian Architecture: Research, Preservation of Monuments / I. E. Grabar. — Moscow, 1969.
40. Danilova, L. V. The Rural Community in Medieval Rus / L. V. Danilova. — Moscow, 1999.
41. Dubrovsky, S. M. Stolypin's Land Reform / S. M. Dubrovsky. — Moscow, 1963.
42. Dudzinskaya, E. A. Slavophiles in Post-Reform Russia / E. A. Dudzinskaya. — Moscow, 1994.
43. Yelichenko, E. B. Stoglav: Research and Text / E. B. Yelichenko. — Moscow, 2000.
44. Zenkovsky, S. A. Russian Old Belief / S. A. Zenkovsky. — Moscow, 2009.
45. Zlatopolsky, D. L. The USSR—A Federal State / D. L. Zlatopolsky. — Moscow, 1967.
46. Zolotukhin, N. M. Joseph Volotsky / N. M. Zolotukhin. — Moscow, 1981.
47. Zubkova, E. Yu. Postwar Soviet Society: Politics and Everyday Life / E. Yu. Zubkova. — Moscow, 2000.
48. Zyryanov, P. N. The Peasant Community of European Russia: 1907–1914 / P. N. Zyryanov. — Moscow, 1992.
49. Illeritsky, V. E. S. M. Solovyov / V. E. Illeritsky; ed. by A. A. Preobrazhensky, Doctor of Historical Sciences. — Moscow: Nauka, 1980.
50. History of Russia from Ancient Times to the Present Day / A. N. Bokhanov, L. E. Morozova, M. A. Rakhmatullin, A. N. Sakharov, V. A. Shestakov; edited by A. N. Sakharov. — Moscow, 2016.
51. History of the Southern and Western Slavs. Vol. 1. The Middle Ages and Modern Times / edited by G. F. Matveev and Z. S. Nenasheva. — Moscow, 2008.
52. Cossacks of the Urals and Siberia in the 18th–20th Centuries: Collection of Scientific Works. Russian Academy of Sciences, Ural Branch, Institute of History and Archaeology; edited by N. A. Minenko. — Yekaterinburg, 1993.
53. Kamensky, Z. A. T. N. Granovsky / Z. A. Kamensky. — Moscow, 1988.
54. Kara-Murza, S. G. Soviet Civilization: From the Great Victory to the Present Day / S. G. Kara-Murza. — Moscow, 2001.
55. Carrer d'Ancoss, E. The Eurasian Empire: History of the Russian Empire from 1552 to the Present Day / E. Carrer d'Ancoss. — Moscow: ROSSPEN, 2007.

56. Kasyanova, K. Features of the Russian National Character / K. Kasyanova. — Moscow, 1993.
57. Kaufman, A. A. Resettlement and Colonization. State Policy and Peasant Land Ownership in Post-Reform Russia / A. A. Kaufman. — Moscow: Librokom, 2012.
58. Kashevarov, A. N. The Orthodox Russian Church and the Soviet State (1917–1922) / A. N. Kashevarov. — Moscow, 2005.
59. Klein, L. S. The Resurrection of Perun: Towards a Reconstruction of East Slavic Paganism / L. S. Klein. — Saint Petersburg, 2004.
60. Kovalchenko, I. D. Stolypin's Agrarian Reform: Myths and Reality / I. D. Kovalchenko. — Moscow, 1992.
61. Koretsky, V. I. The Formation of Serfdom and the First Peasant War in Russia / V. I. Koretsky. — Moscow, 1975.
62. Kostomarov, N. I. Cossacks / N. I. Kostomarov. — Moscow, 1995.
63. Peasant Wars in Russia in the 17th–18th Centuries: Problems, Searches, Solutions. — Moscow: Nauka, 1974.
64. Kutuzov, B. The Secret Mission of Patriarch Nikon / B. Kutuzov. — Moscow: Algoritm, 2007.
65. Lobachev, S. V. Patriarch Nikon / S. V. Lobachev. — Saint Petersburg, 2003.
66. Martin, T. The Empire of "Positive Action." Nations and Nationalism in the USSR, 1923–1939 / T. Martin. — Moscow, 2011.
67. Maul, V. Y. Charisma and Rebellion: The Psychological Nature of Popular Movements in Russia in the 16th–18th Centuries / V. Y. Maul. — Tomsk: TSU Publishing House, 2003.
68. Medvedev, A. The True History of the Russian and Ukrainian Peoples / A. Medvedev. — Moscow, 2015.
69. Milov, L. V. The Great Russian Plowman and the Peculiarities of the Russian Historical Process / L. V. Milov. — Moscow: ROSPEN, 1998.
70. Metropolitan Makarii (Bulgakov). History of the Russian Church / Makarii Metropolitan (Bulgakov). — Saint Petersburg, 1857.
71. Nazarov, V. D. The Peasant Uprising Led by I. I. Bolotnikov and the Polish-Lithuanian Commonwealth / V. D. Nazarov, B. N. Flora // Peasant Wars in Russia in the 17th–18th Centuries: Collection. — Moscow, 1974.
72. The Popular Movement in Russia during the Time of Troubles in the Early 17th Century, 1601–1608 / comp. R. V. Ovchinnikov [et al.]. — Moscow, 2003.
73. Nikitin, N. I. Russian colonization from ancient times to the beginning of the 20th century (historical overview) / N. I. Nikitin. — Moscow, 2010.
74. Nikolsky, N. M. History of the Russian Church / N. M. Nikolsky. — Moscow, 2004.
75. Nikonova, S. I. Spiritual Life of Soviet Society in 1965–1985: ideology and culture / S. I. Nikonova. — Kiev, 2006.

76. Nikonov, V. A. The Collapse of Russia in 1917 / V. A. Nikonov. — Moscow, 2011.
77. Nosov, N. E. The Formation of Class-Representative Institutions in Russia. A Study of Ivan the Terrible's Zemstvo Reform / N. E. Nosov. — Leningrad: Nauka, 1969.
78. Obolensky, D. The Byzantine Commonwealth of Nations. Six Byzantine Portraits / D. Obolensky. — Moscow, 2012.
79. Odintsov, M. I. The Russian Orthodox Church in the 20th Century: History, Relations with the State and Society / M. I. Odintsov. — Moscow, 2002.
80. Oleynikov, D. I. Classical Russian Westernism / D. I. Oleynikov. — Moscow, 1996.
81. The Experience of Russian Modernization in the 18th–20th Centuries / Edited by V. V. Alekseev. — Moscow, 2001.
82. Orlov, I. B. Soviet Everyday Life: Historical and Sociological Aspects of Its Formation / I. B. Orlov. — Moscow, 2010.
83. From Yeltsin to Putin. Three Epochs in the Historical Consciousness of Russians / All-Russian Center for the Study of Public Opinion. — Moscow, 2007.
84. Pipes, R. The Agony of the Old Regime. 1905–1907 / R. Pipes. — Moscow, 2005.
85. Patriotism as a Component of Russia's National Policy: Theory and Practice / Compiled by N. F. Bugay. — Moscow, 2010.
86. Petrusko, V. I. Essays on the History of the Russian Church from Ancient Times to the Middle of the 15th Century / V. I. Petrusko. — Moscow, 2019.
87. Poselyanin, E. The Russian Church and Russian Ascetics of the 18th Century / E. Poselyanin. — Saint Petersburg, 1905.
88. Rogalina, N. L. Collectivization: Lessons from Historical Experience / N. L. Rogalina. — Moscow, 1989.
89. Rogozny, P. G. The Church Revolution of 1917: (The Higher Clergy of the Russian Church in the Struggle for Power in the Dioceses after the February Revolution) / P. G. Rogozny. — Saint Petersburg, 2008.
90. Romanov, B. A. People and Customs of Ancient Rus / B. A. Romanov, 1966.
91. Russian Legislation of the 10th–20th Centuries. Vol. 3. Acts of the Zemsky Sobors / ed. by A. G. Mankov. — Moscow: Legal Literature, 1985.
92. Russian Liberalism. Ideas and People / edited by A. A. Kara-Murza. — Moscow, 2004.
93. Russia. 1913. Statistical and Documentary Reference Book / ed. by A. P. Korelin. — St. Petersburg, 1995.
94. Rubakin, N. A. Russia in Figures. Country. People. Estates. Classes (based on official and scientific research) / N. A. Rubakin. — Saint Petersburg, 1912.

95. Russians in Eurasia in the 17th–19th Centuries / V. Ya. Grosul [et al.]. — Moscow, 2008.
96. Saveliev, E. P. Ancient History of the Cossacks / E. P. Saveliev. — Moscow, 2000.
97. Samarin, Yu. F. Orthodoxy and Nationality / Yu. F. Samarin. — Moscow: Institute of Russian Civilization, 2008.
98. Sinitsyna, N. V. The Third Rome: Origins and Evolution of the Russian Medieval Concept of the 15th–16th Centuries / N. V. Sinitsyna. — Moscow, 1998.
99. Smirnov, I. I. Peasant Wars in Russia in the 17th–18th Centuries / I. I. Smirnov, A. G. Mankov, E. P. Podyapolskaya, V. V. Mavrodi. — Moscow; Leningrad: Nauka, 1966.
100. Smirnov, P. T. Orthodox Shrines and Churches of St. Petersburg / P. T. Smirnov. — Saint Petersburg: Petrogradsky Publishing House, 2018.
101. Smolich, I. K. Russian monasticism 988–1917. The life and teachings of the elders / I. K. Smolich. — Moscow: Church Scientific Center Orthodox Encyclopedia, 1997.
102. S. M. Solovyov and His Era: On the 200th Anniversary / Ed. by A. A. Preobrazhensky, Doctor of Historical Sciences. — Moscow: Nauka, 1980.
103. Solovyov, V. S. On Spiritual Power in Russia / V. S. Solovyov // Collected Works. — Vol. 3. — Saint Petersburg, 1989.
104. Solovyov, V. N. Anatomy of the Russian Rebellion. Stepan Razin: Myths and Reality / V. N. Solovyov. — Moscow, 1994.
105. Stanislavsky, A. L. The Civil War in Russia in the 17th Century: The Cossacks at a Turning Point in History / A. L. Stanislavsky. — Moscow: Mysl, 1990.
106. Tikhomirov, M. N. Ancient Moscow / M. N. Tikhomirov. — Moscow, 1947.
107. Tikhomirov, M. N. Class-Representative Institutions (Zemsky Sobors) in 16th-Century Russia / M. N. Tikhomirov // Tikhomirov, M. N. The Russian State in the 15th–17th Centuries. — Moscow, 1973.
108. Tolochko, P. P. Kievan Rus / P. P. Tolochko. — Kiev, 1996.
109. Tolochko, P. P. The Old Russian Nation: Imaginary or Real / P. P. Tolochko. — Moscow, 2005.
110. Tretyakov, P. N. At the Origins of the Old Russian Nation / P. N. Tretyakov. — Moscow, 1963.
111. Tyukavkin, V. G. Great Russian Peasantry and Stolypin's Agrarian Reform / V. G. Tyukavkin. — Moscow, 2001.
112. Tyumentsev, I. O. The Time of Troubles in Russia in the 17th Century: The Movement of False Dmitry II / I. O. Tyumentsev. — Moscow: Mysl, 2008.
113. Usenko, O. G. The Psychology of Social Protest in Russia since the 17th Century / O. G. Usenko. — Tver: TSU Publishing House, 1994. — Part 1.

114. Fedorov, V. A. The Orthodox Church and the State / V. A. Fedorov // Essays on Russian Culture in the 19th Century; edited by L. V. Koshman. — Moscow, 2000. — Vol. 2.
115. The Phenomenon of Russian Eldership. Examples from the Spiritual Practice of Elders / compiled and with an introduction by S. S. Khoruzhiy. — Moscow: IS RPC, 2006. — 272 p.
116. Philotheus. Letter to Grand Duke Vasily on the correction of the sign of the cross and on Sodom's fornication // Anthology of world political thought: in 5 volumes / Ed. — scientific council. G. Yu. Semigin [et al.]. — Moscow, 1997.
117. Firsov, S. L. Power and Fire. The Church and the Soviet State: 1918 — early 1940s. / S. L. Firsov. — Moscow, 2014.
118. Flora, B. N. Polish-Lithuanian Intervention in Russia and Russian Society / B. N. Flora. — Moscow, 2005.
119. Fomin, V. V. The Varangians and Varangian Rus / V. V. Fomin. — Moscow, 2005.
120. Froyanov, I. Ya. Plunge into the Abyss: Russia at the End of the 20th Century / I. Ya. Froyanov. — Saint Petersburg, 2002.
121. Froyanov, I. Ya. The Beginnings of Russian History / I. Ya. Froyanov. — Moscow, 2001.
122. Khomakov, A. S. Russia's Global Mission / A. S. Khomakov. — Moscow: Institute of Russian Civilization, 2011.
123. Tsimbayev, N. I. I. S. Aksakov in the Public Life of Post-Reform Russia / N. I. Tsimbayev. — Moscow: Moscow State University Press, 1978.
124. Tsimbayev, N. I. Slavophilism. From the History of Russian Social and Political Thought of the 19th Century / N. I. Tsimbayev. — Moscow, 2013
125. Tsimbayev, N. I. Sergei Solovyov / N. I. Tsimbayev. — Moscow: Molodaya Gvardiya, 1990.
126. Tsypin, V. A. History of the Russian Church 1917–1997 / V. A. Tsypin. — Moscow, 1997.
127. Cherepnin, L. V. Zemsky Sobors of the Russian State in the 16th–17th Centuries / L. V. Cherepnin. — Moscow, 1978.
128. Cherepnin, L. V. Introduction. On the study of peasant wars in Russia in the 17th–18th centuries: gaps, searches, solutions / L. V. Cherepnin. — Moscow, 1974.
129. Shelokhaev, V. V. The Liberal Model of Russia's Restructuring / V. V. Shelokhaev. — Moscow, 1999.
130. Shkarovsky, M. V. The Russian Orthodox Church in the 20th Century / M. V. Shkarovsky. — Moscow, 2010.
131. Schmidt, S. O. At the Origins of Russian Absolutism: A Study of the Socio-Political History of Ivan the Terrible's Time / S. O. Schmidt. — Moscow, 1973.

132. Elbakyan, E. S. Religion in Russia. Reference Dictionary / E. S. Elbakyan. — Moscow: Encyclopedia, 2014.
133. Etkind, A. Internal Colonization: Russia's Imperial Experience / A. Etkind. — Moscow: New Literary Review, 2013.
134. Yakubovskaya, S. I. The Development of the USSR as a Union State. 1922–1936 / S. I. Yakubovskaya. — Moscow, 1972.
135. Yanin, V. L. Essays on the History of Medieval Novgorod / V. L. Yanin. — Moscow, 2008.

Publications in scientific journals, collections, and the media

136. Archimandrite Makarii (Veretennikov). The First Patriarch Job and His Time / Makarii Archimandrite (Veretennikov) // Bulletin of the Yekaterinburg Theological Seminary. — 2018. — No. 1. — P. 65.
137. Baturkin, A. The Religious Policy of the Russian Empire in the Second Half of the 19th Century / A. Baturkin // Power. — 2009. — № 2. — P. 4–5.
138. Vasilenko, I. A. Dynamics of political values in the process of mobilization of modern Russia / I. A. Vasilenko // News of Tula State University. Humanities. — 2016. — No. 4. — P. 63–67.
139. Volodikhin, D. M. Metropolitan Dionysius Grammaticus of Moscow and All Russia as the presumed author of the idea of establishing a patriarchal see in Moscow / D. M. Volodikhin // Historical Review. — 2019. — No. 20. — Pp. 28–44.
140. Galimov, T. R. The influence of the Horde on the canonical and legal status of the metropolitan see and the Russian Church in the second half of the 13th — early 14th centuries / T. R. Galimov // Ancient Rus: in time, in personalities, in ideas. — 2017. — No. 8. — P. 435.
141. Gerishtein, I. Z. The factor of messianism in the foreign policy of the USSR / I. Z. Gerishtein // Bulletin of the Vyatka State University of Humanities. — 2017. — No. 4. — P. 52–57.
142. Golitsyn, N. S. Nikolo-Ugreshsky Monastery (excerpts from an essay) / N. S. Golitsyn // Cultural Heritage of Russia. — Moscow, 2013.
143. Golovnev, A. V. Living Border: Cossack Maneuvers in the Space of Colonization (turn of the 16th–17th centuries) / A. V. Golovnev // Tractus aevorum. — Belgorod, 2015.
144. Gorsky, A. A. The Emergence of Russian Statehood and the "Calling of the Varangians" / A. A. Gorsky // Bulletin of Moscow University. Series 8: History. — 2012. — No. 5. — P. 15.
145. Dorskaya, A. A. The legal status of a subject of the Russian Empire at the beginning of the 20th century: the religious aspect / A. A. Dorskaya // News of the Russian State Pedagogical University named after A. I. Herzen. — 2002. — No. 4. — P. 214, 215.

146. Eremin, A. V. The Formation of State and Church Relations in Russia: A Historical and Cultural Analysis / A. V. Eremin // Bulletin of Moscow State University of Culture and Arts. — 2014. — P. 39.
147. Zagraevsky, S. V. On the question of the capital of North-Eastern Rus: Pereslavl-Zalessky under Yuri Dolgoruky, Bogolyubovo under Andrei Bogolyubsky / S. V. Zagraevsky // Materials of the XX Interregional Local History Conference (April 17, 2015). — Vladimir. — 2016. — P. 296–306.
148. Zorin, A. L. The ideology of "Orthodoxy, autocracy, and nationality": an attempt at reconstruction / A. L. Zorin // New Literary Review. — 1996. — No. 26. — Pp. 92–101.
149. Korolev, A. S. On the role of the Varangian princes in the formation of the ancient Russian state / A. S. Korolev // Teacher. XXI century. — 2009. — No. 4. — P. 206–213.
150. Kotychev, D. M. From the history of the formation of statehood in Eastern Europe: "Russian land" in the Middle Dnieper region in the 9th–10th centuries / D. M. Kotychev // Bulletin of the Udmurt University. Series: History and Philology. — 2011. — No. 3. — Pp. 16–25.
151. Kudryavtsev, M. A. V. O. Klyuchevsky's views on the Zemsky Sobors. The ratio of administrative and representative elements in their activities / M. A. Kudryavtsev // Proceedings of the Institute of State and Law of the Russian Academy of Sciences. — 2015. — No. 5. — P. 150.
152. Kudryashev, V. N. The transformation of Slavophilism into Pan-Slavism as a change in the concept of Russian nationalism / V. N. Kudryashev // Bulletin of Tambov State University. — 2012. — No. 364. — Pp. 65–71.
153. Kuliev, F. M. Legal regulation of religious activities in the Russian Empire in the late 18th – early 20th centuries / F. M. Kuliev // Izvestiya SOIGSI. — 2015. — No. 15. — P. 18.
154. Melnik, A. G. The proud people of Rostov: the self-awareness of the inhabitants of Rostov at the end of the 11th and first third of the 13th centuries / A. G. Melnik // Yaroslavl Pedagogical Bulletin. — 2016. — No. 3. — P. 282.
155. Milyukov, P. N.: Historian, Politician, Diplomat / Ed. by V. V. Shelokhaev // Proceedings of the International Scientific Conference (May 26–28, 1999). — Moscow, 2000.
156. Mironov, B. N. The Church and the State Before and After the Russian Revolution of 1917 / B. N. Mironov // Bulletin of St. Petersburg State University. History. — 2020. — Vol. 65. — Issue 2.
157. Michurina, Z. V. The Problem of Spiritual Identity in the Works of P. Ya. Chaadaev and N. Ya. Danilevsky / Z. V. Michurina // Society: Philosophy, History, Culture. — 2017. — No. 8.

158. Myrikova, A. V. "Poets of Slavdom": A. S. Khomyakov and F. I. Tyutchev on Slavic Reciprocity / A. V. Myrikova, B. A. Trokudin // Russian Political Science. — 2018. — No. 6.
159. Nizhnikov, S. A. P. Ya. Chaadaev: From Mythological Image to Real Person / S. A. Nizhnikov // Bulletin of the Russian University of Friendship of Peoples. Series: Philosophy. — 2017. — No. 4.
160. Beloved historian. Timofey Granovsky: a brilliant professor who did not engage in science // Kommersant. Money. — 2016. —№ 40. — P. 43.
161. Olenin, T. S. The problem of classifying Russian religious sectarianism in the Russian Empire / T. S. Olenin // University News. North Caucasus Region. Social Sciences. Appendix. — 2005. — No. 2. — P. 15–16.
162. Osipova, V. V. Russian sectarianism as a form of religious dissent in the pre-revolutionary period / V. V. Osipova // State Administration. Electronic Bulletin. –2019. — No. 76. — P. 4.
163. Panarin, A. A. Implementation of the Bolshevik Party's plans for a world socialist revolution in 1917–1920 / A. A. Panarin // Humanities and Legal Studies. — 2017. — No. 2. — P. 110–115.
164. Patyulina, N. D. The Nikolo-Ugrsky Monastery in the socio-political system of the state / N. D. Patyulina // News of the Russian State Pedagogical University named after A. I. Herzen. — 2008. — No. 82-1. — P. 270–275.
165. Petrusko, V. I. The Moscow Council of 1503 / V. I. Petrusko // Bulletin of the PSTGU Series: History. History of the Russian Orthodox Church. — 2016. — Issue 6. — P. 15.
166. Pivovarov, N. Yu. Soviet Foreign Economic Strategy: Departmental Projects and Bureaucratic Mechanisms (Late 1950s – First Half of the 1960s) / N. Yu. Pivovarov, T. A. Dzhamilov // New Historical Bulletin. — 2019. — No. 4. — P. 55–57.
167. Rudenskaya, T. V. Russian Eldership as a Spiritual Phenomenon of Orthodoxy / T. V. Rudenskaya // Bulletin of Orenburg University. — 2011. — No. 120. — Pp. 15–20.
168. Safonov, A. A. Regulation of the Activities of Non-Orthodox and Non-Christian Denominations by the Ministry of Internal Affairs / A. A. Safonov // Bulletin of Perm State University named after N. A. Nekrasov. — 2006. — No. 5. — P. 32.
169. Skorokhodova, S. I. "The Russian Idea" in the Context of Slavophilism / S. I. Skorokhodova // Science and School, 2012. —№ 4. — Pp. 176–181.
170. Skorokhodova, S. I. The Idea of Slavic Brotherhood in the Works of Representatives of the "Moscow School" / S. I. Skorokhodova // Teacher of the 21st Century. — 2012. — No. 4. — Part 2. — Pp. 250–251.

171. Sopov, A. V. The Origin of the Cossacks: Returning to the Problem / A. V. Sopov // Bulletin of Moscow University. Series 8: History. — 2011. — No. 1. — Pp. 54–65.
172. Ukolova, V. I. The Formation of Early Russian Statehood in the Context of Medieval European Political Genesis / V. I. Ukolova, P. P. Shkarenkov // New Historical Bulletin. — 2016. —No. 4. — Pp. 8–19.
173. Fedyakin, A. V. Political continuity in the image of Russia: history and modern realities / A. V. Fedyakin // Bulletin of Moscow University. Series 12: Political Sciences. — 2009. — No. 1. — Pp. 63–72.
174. Fomina, T. Yu. The Episcopal Structure of Rus during the Mongol-Tatar Invasion of 1237–1240. / T. Yu. Fomina // Zolotoordynskoe Obozrenie. — 2019. — No. 7. — P. 261.
175. Fomina, T. Yu. Bishoprics of Southwestern Rus: stages of formation and development (10th–13th centuries) / T. Yu. Fomina // Christian Reading. — 2016. — No. 6.
176. Fomina, T. Yu. Russian Bishoprics of the Era of Vladimir Svyatoslavich / T. Yu. Fomina // Paleorossiya. Ancient Rus in Time, Personalities, and Ideas. — 2015. — Issue 3.
177. Fomina, T. Yu. The Formation and Development of the Northeastern Russian Bishoprics (late 10th–13th centuries) / T. Yu. Fomina // Paleorossiya. Ancient Rus: in time, personalities, ideas. — 2016. — No. 6. — Pp. 387–392.
178. Friz, G. L. The Church, Religion, and Political Culture at the Twilight of the Old Regime / G. L. Friz // History of the USSR. — 1991. — No. 2. — Pp. 107–118.
179. Khudoley, K. K. The evolution of ideas of world revolution in the politics of the Soviet Union (the era of the Comintern and socialism in one country) / K. K. Khudoley // Bulletin of St. Petersburg State University. Political Science. International Relations. — 2017. — Vol. 10. — Issue 2. — Pp. 151–159.
180. Cherkasov, A. A. Ukrainian nationalism during World War II: nature and manifestations / A. A. Cherkasov, E. F. Krinco, M. Shmigel // Rusyn. — 2015. — No. 2.
181. Chernukha, V. V. Economic and Political-Legal Aspects of Church and Monastic Land Ownership in Russian History / V. V. Chernukha, G. A. Timoshenko // News of Orenburg State Agrarian University. — 2016. — No. 2. — P. 244.
182. Chistyakova, T. L. Slavophiles and Neo-Slavophiles. A. Khomyakov, N. Danilevsky, K. Leontiev / T. L. Chistyakova // Bulletin of Murmansk State Technical University. — 2000. — No. 3. — P. 515–524.
183. Shaposhnik, V. V. Financial Issues at the Stoglav Council / V. V. Shaposhnik // Christian Reading. — 2014. —№ 1. — Pp. 111–112.
184. Shirinyants, A. A. "Internal" Russophobia and the "Polish Question" in 19th-century Russia / A. A. Shirinyants, A. V. Myrikova // Contours of Global Transformations: Politics, Economics, Law. — 2015. — Issue 1.

Sources on electronic media

185. All 13 pre-Mongol churches of Veliky Novgorod and its surroundings. — URL: https://globeofrussia.ru/2016/01/vse-13-domongolskih-hramov-velikogo-novgoroda-i-okrestnostey/ (accessed: 01.05.2021).
186. Ten churches in Pskov on the UNESCO list. Why are they a must-see? — URL: ttps://tass.ru/v-strane/ 6664403 (accessed on 01.05.2021).
187. Dronov, I. E. Kirievsky Ivan Vasilyevich / I. E. Dronov. — URL: https://w.histrf.ru/articles/article/show/kirieievskii_ivan_vasilievich (accessed: 25.01.2021).
188. Zorin, A. Westernizers, Slavophiles, and Others: Debates on Russia's Path / A. Zorin. — URL: https://arzamas.academy/materials/1384 (accessed: 24.01.2021).
189. Iversky Monastery in Valdai. — URL: https:// iveron.ru/iverskaya-ikona-bozhiej-materi/ (accessed on 21.06.2019).
190. Icon of the Dormition of the Mother of God. — URL: https:// pskovo-pechersky-monastery.ru/icon/25-obraz-uspeniya-bozhiej-materi (accessed: 01.05.2021).
191. "Icons Guarding the Russian Land" — 3 icons that saved Russia. — URL: https://moiarussia.ru/ikony-na-strazhe-zemli-russkoj/ (accessed on 31.03.2022).
192. Labanov, S. Fyodor Tyutchev: poet, entrepreneur, political publicist (on the 200th anniversary of the birth of F. I. Tyutchev) / S. Labanov // Internet magazine of the Sretensky Monastery. — URL: https:// pravoslavie.ru/jurnal/031216111111.htm (accessed on 22.02.2021).
193. Venerated icons of the Holy Trinity Alexander Nevsky Lavra. — URL: https://lavra.spb.ru/about/saints-and-shrines/2010-03-31-06-38-16/7-2010-03-31-08-05-18.html (accessed on 27.03.2022).
194. Holy Pafnutiev Borovsky Monastery. — URL: http://www.pafnuty-abbey.ru/about/ (accessed on 22.03.2022).
195. Secularization as a process and phenomenon—types, characteristics, significance. — URL: https://velikayakultura.ru/fenomeny-sovramennoy- kultury/sekul-yarizatsiay-kak-protses-u-fenomen-vidy-cherty-znachenie (accessed: 21.09.2021).
196. Contemporary miracles based on the motives of St. John of Kronstadt.—URL: https://imonspb.ru/sv-prav-ioann-kronshtadtskiy/sovremennyie-chudesa-po-molitvam-sv-prav-ioanna-kronshtadtskogo/ (accessed on 07.05.2021).
197. TransFiguration Monastery. — URL: https://city-yaroslavl. ru/tourism/places/ spaso-preobraxhenskiy-monastyr (accessed: 17.09.2021).

www.ingramcontent.com/pod-product-compliance
Lightning Source LLC
Chambersburg PA
CBHW071205070526
44584CB00019B/2922